Banking Basic$

For Believer$

Darrell G. Wolfe

Bulldog Publications

Published By
Bulldog Publications
Fort Worth, TX

For information, speaking engagements, to contact the author, or
to purchase another copy or find other titles visit our website online at:
"www.DarrellWolfe.Com"

Copyright: © Darrell G. Wolfe 2010
First Edition by Darrell G. Wolfe

ISBN 1453815619
EAN-13 is 9781453815618

~ 3 ~

I would like to thank Jesus,
my constant friend who always leads me.

I would like to thank my wife, Flavia.
She is my Grace and without her constant support
I would not have written this book at all!

Index

$

INTRODUCTION

I have come to the conclusion that many people have little knowledge of banking, the workings of a bank, and the basic facts they need to know in order to navigate these waters smoothly. This is especially frustrating for people today as these topics are often no longer taught in schools, and many parents aren't equipped to train their children on these matters. Many people are left to fend for themselves in a mine field of complicated disclosures and legal regulations.

This work is written first and foremost to the audience of spirit filled believers in the Lord Jesus Christ, and secondly to anyone who would seek to learn the basics of finances and the banking world.

The body of Christ is under mandate through the parable of the talents[1] to act responsibly in the area of finance. Only by treating money God's way, as your servant and not your master will you be able to have truly spiritual use of it. God's plan for money is that it be used to fund and

---

[1] Mathew 25: 14-30

further His Kingdom and provide abundantly for the children (You and Me) that He loves so much.

You must have money and use it accurately in order to do this. The underlying heart of this book and reason for it's existence is found in 2 Corinthians 9:8 *"And God is able to make all grace abound toward you, that you, always having all sufficiency in all things, may have an abundance for every good work."* It is through understanding money and our modern monetary system that we will be able to use it to fund and further the Good News of the Kingdom of God.

Therefore we will discuss the basics of banking to give you a foundation on which you can begin to build a solid financial house. I will introduce you to basic principles to live by. Then I will discuss banking products. I will also discuss some of the pitfalls people find themselves trapped in and how to avoid them. I will then give some tips on getting out of trouble. Finally I have included some supplemental material to help further you're your understanding if you so desire.

* Due to privacy, the stories in this book are not of any one person, but illustrate the types of things real people have gone through.

*Also due to constant changes keep up to date with news releases and watch your banks disclosure mailings, this information is as current as the publish date.

*Some very serious changes are happening in the US Economy. As I wrap up this book the field is set for the US dollar to lose its' status as the reserve currency of the world. The world could in the near future switch to a new currency all together. The stage is set for the end times and the rapture of the church. There is no saying that we may not be using a one world currency before the rapture happens. God's principles work in all situations at all times.

The beautiful thing about this book is that it has been written using principles as well as facts and data. All of the things I teach here could just as easily be applied in any other society where banking occurs, and in any currency. Have faith in God. Pray in the Spirit. Walk in The Blessing. Be empowered to prosper with good success! Darrell G. Wolfe

Section I

Principles

$

1

MONEY

There is a right place, a good place, for money in your life. There is a place where money is not your god but your servant. Money makes a terrible master but a fine servant. If money is your servant than it doesn't matter how much you have, it will never control you.

It takes money to print bibles, tracts, and books. It takes money to translate and print bibles and books into other languages. It takes money to ship those items and get them distributed into other places. It takes money to feed the poor, clothe the naked, and build shelters for the homeless. I had one young man try to tell me he didn't need money, he said that he could go preach one on one anywhere in the world. I thought about that for a long time. He'll still need food, clothing, covering, transportation, bathrooms, etc. Even if he doesn't pay for them someone will have to. So really what he's saying is that he'd rather be burden on others than believe God for provision. It sounds holy, but it's actually selfish.

Let's take a look at a few scriptures that talk about how we are to conduct ourselves in the arena of work:

Deuteronomy 8:7,18

"...For the LORD your God is bringing you into a good land... And you shall remember the LORD your God, for it is He who gives you power to get wealth"

Ephesians 4:28

"...let him labor, working with his hands what is good, that he may have something to give him who has need."

1 Thessalonians 4:11 NIV

"... mind your own business and to work with your hands...so that you will not be dependent on anybody."

1 Thessalonians 4:11 NKJV

"...to mind your own business, and to work with your own hands...that you may lack nothing."

So we can see that God is the one who gives us the power (means and ability) to get wealth. We also see the purpose of work is so that we lack nothing, we are not dependant on anybody, and so that we can give to those in need.

God also wants to be a Father to us! We've known God as Savior, Healer, King, Provider of Needs, but we must know Him as Father. Good Fathers give to their kids. What decent father out there hasn't gotten something for their kid that they did not "need"? What grandparent hasn't gotten something for their grand baby that they did not need? Isn't this the point Jesus made about Father's giving stones to their kids when they asked for bread? He said even evil people don't do that. He is OUR FATHER who gives us richly all things to enjoy[2].

Having said that let us take a look at an example of how not to live. Let us take a look at the story of Edward. He would often attend family meetings in his old car and very seldom wore anything new. When he did buy something "new" it would be from the local thrift store. One day the family got word that he had died. After the funeral was over and things had settled down from a busy week the family all gathered at his house to begin cleaning it out. It was a fine old house, small but quaint.

Upon investigation they found over $68,000 in cash stuffed neatly into the mattress. They found another $35,000 rolled into socks in the dresser. The same story throughout the rest of the house; crevices, couches coffee tables, coffee cans, and even in the freezer, money was stashed everywhere. He had always seemed like the kind of person who was living off of little to nothing. He was always complaining how money was tight and usually only gave cards at Christmas time and for Birthdays, never presents or cash. Eventually over $1.5 million was

---

[2] 1 Timothy 6:17

discovered throughout the house. More money came by the sale of antique furniture. There was another car he owned but rarely drove in the back garage under cover. The car, a 1950 Mercedes in rare like new condition and hardly driven, sold to a collector for over $100,000 dollars. Edward was sitting on, sleeping on, and driving a living fortune. He never did enjoy any of it. He never really used anything to satisfy his basic needs, or the needs or desires of others.

This then brings us to the point of this story. Why have money if you're not going to use it? Money is nothing more than the medium of exchange used to trade time, talent, and resources. Edward had money that he could have used to enjoy life and to help others enjoy it. He chose, instead, to live in fear of loosing it. Money is only worth its ability to help you acquire needs, wants, and desires for yourself and others. What Edward failed to recognize was that true wealth can never be measured in money. It can not be measured in the having of or not having of money.

In Israel today you can find a saying, it is used as a greeting much like "Hello" in the USA. The word is "Shalom". In Arabic the word is "Salem". In English the word is "Peace". The Hebrew definition and meaning of this word is "Nothing Missing, Nothing Broken, Everything Whole and Complete".

Edward failed to see that money without family is not living. Having money and not enjoying it is not living. Having money and being afraid of loosing it is worse than not having it. So the very first thing we must settle for ourselves is: "What money is." & "What it is not."

We've seen what money is not. It is not security. Money is NOT: happiness, or true wealth by itself. We all know of people who have a lot of money but are miserable. You may know them personally or know of them.

In 1 Timothy 6:6-10, we see that godliness with contentment is great gain but the love of money is a root of all kinds of evil. Where does this contentment come from? How do we avoid this money anxiety? Philippians 4 gives us our answer: "...be anxious for nothing, but through prayer and supplication with thanksgiving let our requests be known to God. Prayer and Supplication, in Greek, literally mean General Requests and Specific Requests. It is through these requests with thanksgiving that we can do ALL things through Christ, (the Anointed One and His Anointing). What thanksgiving? We thank God not only for what he has already done... we thank Him in advance for giving us what we asked for, believing that He will and that it's already done. (Mark 11:24 and 1 John 5:14-15)

Jesus told us, in Matthew 6:24-34, that we are not to worry about money meeting our needs but to seek God's right order of doing things and all the rest of this we need, want, and desire would be added to us through Him!

Money is a tool, nothing more or less. There was a day in world history that we all used a system of trade. It is now called the "Barter System."

~Barter System~

If I owned cattle and you owned chickens, I could trade my milk for your eggs. Thus; in many trades we all get what we need. The problem is: if I need eggs, but you don't want milk than I have to go trade for something else you do want to then trade for your eggs. This system, although simple, was cumbersome and awkward.

Over time people would trade jewels, stones and metal for products and services. Eventually governments printed coins from metals (usually gold) with very specific logo's to use as currency. As time went on they began to use printed paper, in addition to the metal coins. As people gathered and collected more and more coins and paper there arose the need to store it somewhere safe. If you leave it in your house and then leave, someone could come and take it, or it could be burnt down. All the gathering would have been lost.

~Banking System~

This was the birth of the bank. A bank in its simplest form keeps your money safer from theft and disaster, and pays you for letting them use it. The bank benefits by lending the money to folks who need it in return the borrower pays it back plus interest. Interest is money you pay for borrowing money, and it is also money you earn for letting the bank use your money.

Jesus mentioned the banking system. He awarded the one who had turned his five talents into ten. He told the one who had dug a whole and buried the money God gave him that he should have, at the very least, turned it in to the bank for interest. (Matthew 25:27)

~Today~

Today all over the world, and especially here in the USA, there are many financial institutions. In recent decades changes have been made that allow for more competition and convenience. Up until the last few decades you purchased stock market products through investment firms, insurance through insurance companies, banking either through banks, savings and loans, or credit unions. Law changes over the last few decades have allowed one company to offer all in one services, to a degree. The competition has added fresh air to the market and created new products and services. It has also made it easier to do one stop shopping.

These same law changes caused a new development; The National Bank. Most banks for the greater history of the world were local. They had a few branches here and there. Having a bank in two states required partnership between banks. Law changes now allow for banks to have branches in more than one state. This created the national bank. There are laws restricting how big one bank can be. However many banks are getting larger, adding more and more access to banking wherever you go.

~Time~

"Time is money!" That saying has been rolling around for a long time. What does it mean? There are many resources in the world. Trees can be regrown. Oil although running low will last a very long time, in fact we haven't even tapped all the known resources for oil. Money when lost can be remade. In the bible, Job lost everything he had and ended up with double what he had at first in the end.[3]

---

[3] **Job 42:10**

Time, on the other hand, cannot be renewed. It's true that God operates outside of time. It is even possible for Him to catch you up if you've fallen behind. It is possible for him to slow, reverse, or even stop time to accomplish something[4].

Ultimately, though, you have been given 24 hours a day, and 365 days a year on our common calendar. When you spend a day worrying about what you're going to do about a problem that has come along you will not get that day back. You could invest your time in confessing the Word over that problem and meditating on what God says about it and thanking Him in advance for his provision. That would be a wiser use of your time.

The time you spend will be spent. We even use the term "spent" in reference to time because we understand that it is valuable. Time is a resource, a commodity.

Five people working on a project will make it happen faster than one person could on their own. That is because time has been duplicated in the efforts of many. When you are hired to work at a grocery store to push carts, you are effectively hired for your time. The owner or manager of that store could go and push the carts if he

---

[4] **Joshua 10:13, Habakkuk 3:11, 2 Kings 20:11, and Isaiah 38:8**

wanted to. However he would not be able to attend to the paperwork and decision-making he needs to do. So he hires you to duplicate his efforts and maximize his own time. You then trade your time for a pay check. You may get paid little or much, but you traded your time for money.

So why do we think it's so important to trade our time, which we cannot get back, for money which they print everyday and which decreases in value everyday? We do this because money is useful to us. Money is a tool. It's a hammer or screw driver. A person can use a hammer in anger to break an expensive crystal vase or calmly and skillfully use it to drive a nail into the frame of a new house being built. One use is appropriate and one is not. Both can be done by the same person. The heart of the person holding the hammer will determine the use of that hammer. In the same manner the heart of the person using money will determine the use of that money.

Many people inside and outside of churches throughout America quote a bible verse that says: "Money is the root of all evil." This is actually a miss-quote. The bible doesn't say money is the root of all evil. It says, in 1 Timothy 6:10, that the LOVE of money is the root of all KINDS of evil. To love money is to trust money for your security, this is always wrong. It will always lead to trouble. You can commit this crime without ever owning a dime. The next time you find yourself worried about bills, or how you are going to feed your family, or get a roof over your head, or clothe yourself, you can be assured you are committing this subtle and insidious crime. Worrying about money IS serving money. (Matthew 6:24-25)

Your purpose for money is what you can use it for. The wise use of wealth is more important that the wise use of a hammer. The man with his hammer crafts a fine home for the people he builds it for. The wise use of wealth crafts lifestyles, homes, jobs, provision, food, clothing, joy, peace, and most importantly provides the tools needed to spread the Gospel of a loving Jesus to a dying world.

In Luke 22:7-14 Jesus is given the use of a man's home for his last supper. In Acts 16:14-15 Paul is given the use of a woman's home to preach the gospel. In I Kings 17:8-10 we see God use a widow woman's gift to Elijah to provide for both him and herself and her son through a deadly drought. Over and over we see God provide through people.

~Preachers Money~

Have you ever noticed how easy it is for someone to think that a sports person is being shafted when he is offered less than 10 million for a contract, but that same person starts to balk and squawk if he hears of a Pastor making 1 million? If you value The Word as more valuable than any other thing on the planet, and your Pastor handles The Word and delivers it to you week in and week out faithfully, than you should make absolutely sure that your Pastor is WELL taken care of. The Pastor SHOULD be among the highest paying callings in the world because he or she deals with The Word. If you don't agree than you are telling us that The Word is NOT the highest priority in your life, plain and simple.

~Conclusion~

Money is not evil. Money is not good. The heart of the holder determines its value. Money is a tool. Money is a representation of your time, therefore you should be paid what your time is worth. Money is worthless unless it has direction and purpose. Money is essentially paper or numbers on a screen. Money is worth only what people value it to be worth. Money is a hammer and chisel. It will destroy or it will create master pieces depending on the hands that wield it.

So now that we have settled where money came from and what it's good for, let us move on to the practical applications for it.

If you are interested in a deeper look at what the Word of God says about wealth for the believer I suggest you start with a book from Kenneth Copeland Ministries: "The Laws of Prosperity[5]".

---

[5] www.kcm.org

$

2

TITHE

In order to start on the right foot we must now talk about the tithe. Simply put tithe is 10%. The key verse to look at when discussing the tithe is Malachi 3:8-12. God says here that not tithing is equal to robbing God. It is interesting to note that this is the only place in the bible God offers man a test or trial of his goodness. Go ahead, God says, test me… try me out… see if I'm faithful to my Word. God knows that money is tied to core matters of the heart. Jesus said that where your treasure is, your heart will be also. (Matthew 6:21 and Luke 12:34)

~Gross VS Net~

What about this 10%? Is that gross or net? Malachi also answers this for us. Bring in the WHOLE tithe. Deut. 14:22 tells us to tithe on all your increase. All means All and that's All All means. For a moment consider what you are really asking in this question. Should I give God 10% of the money I made before or after the government took their cut, and I sent some to my 401K, and I paid for medical deductions, etc etc… Does the government come first or does God? If God is first, that means first. Before anything is removed, God is first.

~Law~

But that is old covenant law, we are not under the Law? Right? Yes we are not under the law. No tithing is not limited to the law. Actually the tithe predates the law. Genesis 14:20 shows us that Abraham paid tithe to Melchizedek after being blessed by God through Him. The law didn't come until Moses who is a distant descendant of Abraham. Moses did not come for well over 400 years later.

In fact Hebrews tells us that Jesus himself receives our tithes. (Hebrews 7:8) The only thing Jesus ever commended the Pharisees on was paying the tithe. (Matthew 23:23)

~God First~

In case you still felt there was room for doubt let us take a look at the very first sin. Genesis Chapters 1-3. God places Adam and Eve in the midst of a vast and fruitful planet. He plants a Garden in the east with instructions to then take the seed and reproduce the Garden on the rest of the planet. He blesses them with Dominion and Authority. All they put their hand to will prosper. He asks one thing in return. He reserves one tree and its fruit. He asks for this to remain His and His alone. This is Adams tithe. He is to take its fruit to God and God alone. He is not instructed not to touch it; that is Eve's twisting of God's words. He is instructed not to eat it.

Essentially, one could determine through looking at the commands given later in scripture, God's plan was for Adam to bring him the fruits of this tree as tithe, offering, and love. God would fellowship and commune with Adam over this and take time to instruct him in matters of life. Truly God didn't mind Adam knowing the difference between good an evil. He created and wanted Adam in HIS own image. God wanted Adam to learn from HIM and not through his own experience of good and evil.

Had Adam left the serpent, stopped Eve from talking to him (since he was there with her), and gone to God... Adam could have asked God about good and evil and He would have told him. Not tithing is always a matter of not trusting God to meet EVERY need, want, and desire. Not tithing is saying: "I'll do this on my own... for myself... I'll be my own provider."

~God's Lease~

Jesus makes this interesting comparison regarding mans lease over the things of God. God the Father, in this story, is likened to a vineyard owner. He sent servants to the vine dressers who turned to beat and kill them. Then He sent his own Son, who was also killed. Jesus tells us that they will be thrown out, and God will lease the vineyard to others. (Matthew 21:40-42)

Adam's first sin is touching that which belonged to God. God created this planet for mankind. He didn't need a planet. In fact, He has many of them. He created this earth for man. The tithe is man's mortgage or lease on the planet. This gives man the rightful use of this property. God is the landowner or Leaser. Man is the renter or leasee. When a man or woman fails to bring God His fruit first he is in danger of breaking lease. God serves notice that only curse and death will follow this course of action. Why?

This lease agreement is an agreement of blessing. To remove yourself from the blessing is to enter the curse by choice. The entire planet is under the curse due to Adam's disobedience. It is the flow of the world's system. It is the blessing, through contact and contract with God, that shields and protects you from the curse. Jesus redeemed us from the curse (Galatians 3:13). It is His blood that keeps us redeemed. He permanently reestablished a covenant between God and Man. This covenant is between God and Jesus so it cannot be broken. It is entered through believing in and on Jesus. Once entered, however, there are terms and conditions.

Obedience, will bring greater degrees of the protection of the blessing. Failing to love your brother may not keep you from heaven when you die, although it could progress to that. However failing to love is a failure to obey and it will cause the curse to operate in your life. So it is with the tithe. It is a connector to God's ways of doing things. It connects you to His blessing. It is a heart matter. The tithe connects you to trusting God for ALL your provision. Failure to tithe is failure to trust. God's not asking you to give so he can take 10% from you. He is asking you to give so he can bless the 90% and bring more to you by increasing the 90%!

~Promise of Blessing~

What is God's promise if we obey him in bringing in the tithe? God says that he will open up the windows of heaven and pour out blessing we cannot contain. This is the same blessing he gave Adam in Genesis 1:28. It is the same blessing then given to Abraham in Genesis 14:18-20. It is the same blessing listed in detail for us in Deut. 28. The curse is listed there also, but only as a result of disobedience. God's heart and passion is to bless us. Only when we disobey are we forcing ourselves to enter and live under a curse.

What happens to a person who fails to pay the rent? I can tell you. I once chose to pay my car note over my rent. I thought the car was more important. I ended up living in that car for about 6 months. Did God want me to live in a car? No He didn't. Was it His will? Was He trying to teach me something? Was He trying to humble me? Why was I tight on funds at that time? I was living in disobedience over some other instructions He had given me. God isn't out to cause bad things to happen to teach you a lesson. He laid it out plain and simple.

God gives us a clear choice in life. He tells us that there are blessing and cursing, life and death. Then He gives a hint, which is His choice; "Choose Life" (Deut. 30:19). Sounds like a no brainer, but this choice often means obeying God when it doesn't feel like it's good. Tithe is a major area for many, but it brings the Blessing.

~THE Blessing~

The blessing of God is the power to get wealth, among other things. It is the power to prosper: spirit, soul, body, mind, financially, socially, etc... In all areas of life, the Blessing invades and creates fruitful environments. The blessing on Joseph saved two nations from starvation. (Genesis 41) The Blessing on Issaac caused him to sow during famine and reap a 100 fold return. (Genesis 26) The Blessing was on Jesus who multiplied fish and loaves for over 5,000 men plus women and children, on two occasions. (John 6 and Matthew 15). Over and over God used blessed people to provide for others. Hebrews 11 lists a hall of fame full of people that obeyed God and operated under the blessing.

The tithe connects you to the blessing. The tithe is only the beginning. God also promises special blessings for those who gives to the poor (Proverbs 19:17), and He has a special place in His heart for those in need. (Deut 10:17-19) We say that those who give to these classes of people are sowers. S.O.W. = Strangers, Orphans and Widows. In Philippians 4 we learn that giving to an anointed ministry doing the Work of God in the earth connects us to their anointing and increases our account with God.

~Heavenly Accounting~

This brings up another interesting point to consider when tithing and giving. We have an account with God. Jesus referred to it when He talked about storing treasure in heaven. Paul referred to it in Philippians 4.

In banking; a checking or savings account is known as a "Demand Deposit Account". This means you have placed money in deposit there but expect to be able to place a demand on that money at any time. This is how it is with God.

We add to that account through every act of obedience and giving to God. We place a demand on that account by asking and believing. We place our treasure there through giving and sowing of our time, talent, and treasure. Jesus told a rich young ruler in Matthew 19 that he should give to the poor... the young man didn't stick around to hear that there was a 100 fold return on that investment. There is no way to ever drain the heavenly account you have because it is increasing beyond the earth's capacity to use it. This is why God said he could open up the windows of heaven and pour out the blessing which you cannot contain. It is however, available for use at a moments notice and with the demand slip called Faith.

~Obedience~

Tithing may be hard at first. I had given off and on throughout my life. When I had rededicated my life to Jesus as Lord and Savior, I decided that I was going to take Him seriously for the first time in a long time. I found in the Word that tithing was not optional. I started by giving ten percent of what I had. I noted that within the first month I went from constantly negative in my accounts to having a little left over. I thought that this was quite remarkable.

I noticed that on months I did not tithe, the devourer came and what I thought I kept I lost. Those months I did tithe, things just went smoother. I later went on to learn about tithing on my gross income and not my net. This required more thought, because I actually had to look at each paycheck to determine what I had made before taxes and deductions. This had the side benefit of knowing what was really happening on my checks and taking control of it. I found out that I could put money in my 401K and less would go to taxes. Essentially I could pay myself instead of the government.

I also started to increase in income. I got better raises. I found money in the oddest places. I also found it easier to stay at one job longer. In one instance I really needed money to register a car and God brought more than enough just a week before it was due.

Tithing will not always be easy. But it doesn't belong to you. It is God's. Make up in your mind right now that tithe comes first no matter what.

~Challenges to Obedience~

For some people that may not be possible. Suppose you are a woman who has just learned about the tithe and you want to obey God. Your Husband (Or wife if you are a man) is not in agreement with this. Find something to give. If you get an allowance, or certain amount to spend for groceries, tithe on that. If you have $5 in your pocket, give some of it to God. Start where you are. You could even challenge the spouse. "We do this for three months. And if we are not better off than we stop." Many have given this challenge to faithless spouses to have the spouse then say at the end of three months: "Whatever it is... keep it up!!"

Whatever your situation, God knows your heart. Start with what you have. Show yourself faithful and God will do the same. This is a heart matter more than a letter of the law matter.

~Proper Tithe~

There is actually more to tithing than dropping money in a bucket. God actually lays out a method to the tithe. You could say it comes with an instruction manual. This is found at length in Deut. 26:1-15, Specifically in 13-15.

[13] *then you shall say before the LORD your God: 'I have* **removed the holy tithe from my house, and also have given them to**

the Levite, the stranger, the fatherless, and the widow, according to all *Your commandments which You have commanded me;* ***I have not*** ***transgressed Your commandments****, nor have I forgotten them.* [14] ***I*** ***have not eaten any of it when in mourning, nor have I removed any*** ***of it for an unclean use, nor given any of it for the dead.*** *I have* *obeyed the voice of the LORD my God, and have done according to all* *that You have commanded me.* [15] ***Look down from Your holy*** ***habitation, from heaven, and bless*** *Your people Israel and the land* *which You have given us, just as You swore to our fathers, "****a land*** ***flowing with milk and honey.****"'*

This was written to the physical people of Israel. What application does this have for those in the new covenant who are the spiritual Israel?

~Remove the Tithe~

First of all we must remove the tithe! This means don't wait until last minute, after the bills are paid and hope there is some left over to tithe with. The tithe comes first before anything else is paid for or paid on. One great way of doing this, and something I have been doing for a while now, is actually set up a separate account for the tithe and offering. If your payroll department will allow split direct deposit you can have 10% or more automatically sent to this special purpose account. You won't even have to think about separating for yourself. You can write a check, take out cash, or use your card, however you normally give from this account knowing the money has already been separated unto God for the work of God in the earth. You may want to try doing 12% or 14% as the direct deposit will only use after tax money for the percentage. If you are tithing on your gross you will need a higher percentage to come out right. A little too much is good too because tithing is the starting place of giving not the max. You may want to allow this account to build up so that you can use the excess as an offering amount. Maybe the church has a building project, or maybe you will meet someone God wants you to reach out and bless. You have already set yourself up to participate by letting this account build up on the side.

~Obey God~

We also see that the tithe must also be accompanied by obedience to other areas of God's Word. Walking in strife, unforgiveness, or any other area of sin will cancel out the benefits of the tithe. Again looking to Jesus' words to the Pharisees (Matthew 23:23); He said you ought to have done these (tithe of the first fruits of all their increase) without neglecting the other more weightier matters (Justice, Mercy, and Faith).

~Don't Eat It~

Do not eat your tithe. This will come as a hard saying, but yes the tithe comes before groceries too. This means you cannot allow a tight month to dictate to you whether or not you will tithe by saying: "Oh well, things are really tight this month... we cannot afford to give this month... God knows our hearts... He understands... we'll just start again next month."

This sounds logical but it is certain death to next months finances. Saying this is exactly the same as saying: "God, we don't really trust you to meet our needs, which includes feeding us. We believe you religiously, but not in practical matters where it counts." Acting in fear, which is what not tithing is caused by, always connects you to the curse and you will find that next month will be tighter than this month. I know from personal experience that when you feel like you cannot afford to tithe, the truth is you cannot afford not to tithe.

~Confess the Tithe~

This passage also shows us the most important and most overlooked matter in the tithe: Confession. God is not just asking for us to put money in a bucket. That alone doesn't connect you to the blessing. In fact you can put 10% of your income in a bucket and still not see any blessing. Tithing is a covenant matter. It connects you to the covenant blessing. You didn't get married without using your words to connect you to marriage. You said some things. If you open a checking account you will sign a document saying that you have read and agreed to the terms and conditions. Confessing your tithe to God is a way of connecting you to His blessing through tithing. Say some things about it. You may even want to take communion with your family, which is another covenant rite. Take a few minutes together either before church or on pay day and talk about the tithe. You could say something like the following modern version:

"Jesus; thank you for your sacrifice! Thank you for the cross. Your blood and broken body redeemed us from the curse. Thanks to you we are free from the bondage of sickness, disease, poverty, lack, sin, and death. We were once under a curse which rules the world's system. Thanks to you, Jesus, we are free! We accept everything you redeemed us from and redeemed us to. We plead your blood over our household. We say we are blessed going in and blessed going out. We are blessed in our bodies and in our bank accounts. We thank you for using us to be a blessing to countless others. We declare divine encounters this month. The windows of heaven are open to us and we are free from the devourer. Thank you. Glory to God!" Then pray some. Praise God. Sing some songs or worship. Adore Him. Do this every payday, if not more often.

This time of confession, prayer, and praise will open up your mind and thought life to meditate on his word and promises. When disaster strikes and the enemy attacks you will have spent time building in yourself a fortress of trust in God. You will be able to say like Paul: None of these things move me (Acts 20:24)! His promise is a land flowing with Milk and Honey. He tells us that land will require faith and fight[6]. It will not be given to us without a fight. There will be enemies to our progress and increase. We will move on in faith. From time to time people will come along trying to move us off of our land and rightful place. We must stand strong in faith. Temptations, trials, and other distractions will not move a true tither, connected to the covenant of blessing. The money could drain and houses fall down and the tither knows, as God did with Job, that double is coming!

~Offering~

You may also want to consider in addition to your tithe a set offering amount every month. Many long time tithers have gone on to make a 20% or more their

---

[6] Joshua 1, 1 Timothy 1:18 & 6:12, 2 Timothy 4:7

minimum. 10% to the church and 10% to ministries and work of God elsewhere. God blesses giving. If you aren't there yet you could start with $5. Choose, through prayer, a place you want to begin sowing/giving to. Maybe there is a minister that you learn from that isn't at your church, sow the $5 into that ministry. Maybe there is an orphanage or elderly home that you feel a strong attachment to. Find a place to start, let God lead you.

Suppose you feel that having too much is a bad thing. It isn't, God wants to overflow your cup according to psalms 23. But suppose you do. You see the world hurting and feel bad for wanting too much. Go ahead and believe god for a $1,000,000 a year. Then live on $50,000. That leaves you $950,000 a year to meet the needs of other people. Who told you that you had to keep it? That way you are GIVING 95% of your income and living on 5%! How's that for Godly math? According to the pattern God shows in the bible, you would not be able to do that long without seeing a significant increase in your income. Go ahead, believe God for TOO MUCH. That is the only way you can participate in meeting the needs of others. That is the principle of 2 Corinthians 9:8. Have too much so that you can have to give.

Now don't take this to mean that you should go give your entire paycheck away today... God may require obedience but He also requires wisdom. Faith comes in the form of seed. You start with the faith you have and work it. Like a muscle or plant, time and patience will cause it to grow. Start where you are, give what you have to give, and watch it multiply over time. Challenge yourself to give more over time, according to your faith. Romans 12:2 says to take time to renew your mind. Then you will be able to test and approve God's will. This includes His will in the area of Giving. Verse 3 tells us to not think that we are beyond where we are. We should not think we are higher or lower than we are, but judge ourselves soberly. This way we can operate at the level of faith we have, practice it, push through it like working weights in a gym. This causes us to know where we are in our faith walk with God and it allows us to know where the next level is too.

If you work 10 pound weights and they are hard at first, work them awhile. In time you find the weights become easier to lift. Soon you can work 20 pounds, then 50. So it is with God. You may find that committing to tithe takes all the faith you can muster. Soon it becomes easier, then routine. Eventually you don't question it or even think about it, it's just natural. At first you may find that sowing an extra $5 is hard, but as you pray God begins to show you that you spend $20 a month on random things you don't need and maybe even didn't want that much. Maybe the whole $20 is spent on one thing or several things.

Over time God will ask you to push yourself in this area of giving. Over time he will ask you to set goals for your giving. Just like working weights in a gym; the goals will seem tough at first and become easier over time. I know one man who committed to giving in every church service he attended, even if it was just $1 he gave every service. Soon he was giving Sunday and Wed and special events. He progressed to a set amount, say $5 each service. Last I heard he was sowing $100 each service and was looking to increase that. His life and business has increased exponentially over time and there is a direct correlation between his increase in giving and his increase in life at every turn. The increase in giving always came before the increase to his financial life.

Decide for yourself where you are in life. Pray it out. Remember that there is no condemnation in God (Romans 8:1). So if you feel bad for not being able to give what you want to, you are on the wrong track. 2 Corinthians 9:7 says:

[7] Each of you should give what you have decided in your heart to give, not reluctantly or under compulsion, for God loves a cheerful giver.

So pray it out, find what you have peace about in your heart, not your head! Give cheerfully. Every time the offering basket comes by your hand, even if you are not giving in that service, you may even want to practice saying: "I LOVE to give!" It will help build inside of you the heart of a giver.

~Reminders~

So remember, tithe is not optional, giving is a connection to the blessings of God. Giving causes increase in your life. Tithe on your gross income, put God first, secure your lease and connection to the blessings of God. Fill your heavenly account. Remove the tithe immediately and separate it from your other money. Walk in obedience in other areas of life. Don't eat the tithe. Confess the Word of God over your giving. Finally pray about what God would have you to do in order to participate in giving over and above your tithe.

$

3

BANKS

Understanding the banking system can seem like a daunting task to the outsider. I talked to an engineer once. He said that he held a masters degree, worked in the field for 30 years and could build me a nuclear lab if I needed one, but just couldn't quite grasp financial matters. I was able to demystify the concerns he had in the hour we talked. He indicated that lacking information is what kept him from making the best use of his accounts. It is not necessary for you to understand ALL the intricacies of the banking business in order to take advantage of the products and services they offer. Simple basics will take you far.

~Case Study: Robert~

Let's take a look at the case study of a person who did things right. We'll call him Robert. He started working part time when he was 15 years old while going to high school. He saved up money for things he wanted. He graduated from high school just before he turned 18.

Robert was on the way to the beach with his friends to drink beer and surf on the beach. He told them to go on ahead of him so he could step into his bank and open a new account. They all laughed at him but he went on his way. As they were at the beach he went into the bank and opened a brand new product the bank was offering through the government called an IRA. They said that he would be guaranteed 10% until he turned 59 ½ years old. So he put in $2000 dollars and let it ride. Several decades latter that IRA CD is worth more than $48,000.

Robert's next great decision is that he bought an old car for cash. He then made payments to himself until he could buy his next car for cash. When he was ready to buy his first home he made sure to shop around and buy the home that was right. He made sure the payments were far under his comfort zone. If he could afford a payment of $1200 he bought a house with a payment of $950. Then he made the $1200 payment anyway and paid his house off years early. Robert is now worth more than 3 million dollars. He now owns four homes, three are debt free and one has a small amount owed on it.

What is more remarkable about Robert is that he still works as a cashier and has never made more than $18 dollars an hour. He simply made many small and wise steps along the way that opened up a world of freedom.

What is the secret to Robert's success? He said no to something today, in order to say yes to something tomorrow. In banking we call that a "Tradeoff". Since he didn't borrow in order to obtain the majority of what he has, he isn't struggling to make the payments on it all. Therefore, he is free to enjoy what he has without concern about it.

~Banking Products~

What do I mean when I say "products" in reference to a bank? Most people think of food, or clothing, or toys when they hear the word products. So what does it mean for a bank to sell a product?

In the financial industry every account or service is a product. A checking account is a product and an ATM card is a product. Unbeknownst to some people, there are various types of products offered by the banks. Most banks offer more than one type of checking account for example. One checking may come with free check orders, or discounts on other services offered by the banks. Some checking accounts earn interest. Usually the more money you keep in the bank the more benefits you will receive on other products and services such as: free checks, discounts on fees, and more. The banks typically reward a commitment on your part. Sometimes the bank may be more likely to give you a loan if you've been with them for 30 years, than if you've never worked with them before, because they are able to prove your established history.

Let's take a look at some of the various products that are offered by the banks and a short description of what they do.

~Checking~

The most basic of all banking products; the checking account is for the daily or frequent withdrawals, bills, and shopping. Some people even keep one account for bills and a second for shopping to keep expenses separate, or to keep better track of their spending. Many keep one account for personal use and another for personal but business related expenses. People who own property may keep a special account just for the deposits of rent checks and rental expenses. Too many accounts and you may just confuse yourself. However it can be nice to keep certain things separate so you don't spend your bill paying money at your favorite clothing store!

~Savings~

The Savings Account is typically where you want to keep anything beyond your monthly used budget. This is an account that usually, but not always, earns a higher interest than the checking.

There is really a more important reason to keep money here than interest though. Primarily the principle of "out of sight, out of mind" is applied here. Experts typically agree you should work towards keeping 6-9 months of income set aside in a savings account. This would cover you if you were to be laid off, or experience an injury, or any number of unexpected circumstances.

For the believer we expect the favor and protection of God at all times. However wisdom will help us recognize that we are not always at the top of our game, and can sometimes open the door for an attack of the enemy to slip through. Being prepared for what may come your way is an act of faith as well.

Save don't store. Another even more important reason to save, as believers, is to have a seed bin. We must have a place where we have dedicated money aside to sow into the Word of God and the Lives of Others. S.O.W. Strangers Orphans and Widows, need us to look out for them (Deut 10:17-19). We as believers are their salt and light. We are their preservative and warmth in a world out to take them down.

~CD~

There is another type of savings account called a CD. CD stands for Certificate of Deposit, it's also known as a Time Account. Whichever term the bank uses the idea is the same. You put money in, and commit to leaving it there for a specific amount of time, in return the bank pays you a higher rate of interest.

This is where you want to keep any of the savings you plan on not touching for 6 months or more. I've talked to more people than I can count who have let $60,000 or more sit in a savings account for years on end earning 2-4% LESS than a CD would have at the same bank. Don't ignore your financial matters. It's harder to work money than it is to work for money, but keeping it serving you rather than you serving it will pay off in the long run.

~Debit Cards~

There are two ways to use your card. If there is no VISA/Master Card logo on your card then it is called an ATM card. You may use it at ATM's to withdraw cash. You may also use it as stores or merchants that take debit cards. When you are at the grocery store and the machine asks you to press "Debit or Credit" you will select debit and enter your P.I.N. Your P.I.N is your Personal Identification Number. This type of transaction is known as a Point Of Sale Purchase, and may post to your account with the description of POS. These will nearly always post to your account the same business day you do them.

If you have a VISA or Master Card Logo on your card than you will also have the option of pressing Credit. When the card has this logo it is called a Check Card. When you press "Credit" at the machine at the grocery store the purchase will still come from your checking account. Instead of that purchase going to a charge card account to be paid later, it will come directly from your checking account. It's a replacement for writing a check.

~Checks~

Paper checks are the oldest form of payment. You typically get a box of checks that hold about 100-200 checks, separated into smaller pads.

You write the person you are paying, the amount both as a number (1) and as a handwritten amount (one), then you sign the bottom.

Depending on how it's processed this check once deposited by the person you wrote it to may take anywhere from 0 to 10 business days to clear, not including weekends or holidays.

Check 21 _Confusing for check writers: There is a new law called Check21. All banks must take an image copy of the original check and typically then destroy the original. This makes all checks electronic. Because that image is then sent to clear the check. Merchants, especially Credit Card companies, don't usually bother depositing the check you mail. They "convert" the check to an electronic item and send it through. This has become a hybrid between a check and a card purchase. As time goes on it will become increasingly less likely you will be able to retrieve an image copy of the checks because companies find it faster and cheaper to convert the checks and send them through as "converted checks". This way instead of being sent through the normal process they are sent through an automated process known as ACH.

~ACH~

This is an electronic check. ACH stands for Automated Clearing House. This is when items are submitted electronically rather than by paper. This includes checks that are "converted checks". It also includes "Pay by Phone", "E-Pay" and "Auto-Pay". It also known as a "Pre-authorized debit." Companies obtain, hopefully from you, your routing and account number and submit an electronic draft from your account. You may have asked them to take payments automatically, by phone, online, or on a form you filled out.

* Note on ACH: *Companies are notorious for creating havoc on accounts through ACH. It's only a matter of time before they take the wrong amount, on the wrong date, and cause overdrafts and find a reason to call it your fault. Don't expect your bank to be MUCH help* *here. They MAY be able to fix it, or may not. I strongly recommend either staying clear of these types of payments entirely or opening an account JUST for these type of payments separate from your normal accounts. I don't care how long you've been with them or how nice they are, it only takes one error to create months of work and headache for you.* **Don't do it if you can help it.**

~Online~

Internet banking is the safest, easiest way, to keep track of your finances. Due to bad media and urban legends online has gotten a bad rap. People often think that by signing up for online they are more open to hacking. The fact is that most hackers aim at large data computers, like the banks computers, which your information will be on whether you ever sign up for online or not.

Numbers and statics vary constantly, but on average today less than 5% of all bank fraud is through information **obtained** electronically. More than 90% of fraud is **committed** electronically, but this is after getting your information through a physical means. Some ways your information is usually obtained are: Stolen checks, or finding your lost checks, stolen wallet, car broken into, or scams to trick you into revealing your information causing you to participate in the information leak.

Online is the safest, fastest way to keep a hold of your banking. Most banks offer Bill Pay, Online Statements, Spending Reports, and more.

~Bill Pay~

This is an online service intended to help you pay your bills. It's the new version of check writing. You input all the people you pay whether it's a one time payment or every month. The bank sends the payment for you and even pays for the postage. You can make a payment to a person or a business. You can make payments just once, or you can set them up to send automatically every month. This is usually free for most accounts at most banks.

~Insurance~

Almost everyone knows about Auto Insurance because in most states you cannot register your car without having it. There are many other types of insurance. Renters and Home Owners both cover your belongings in case something should happen to your home/apartment. Life covers your family in case you pass away. They even have Pet Health insurance now, to cover your pets' hospital/vet bills. Often times the insurance provider will offer discounts for having more than once policy with them. For example having Auto and Renters may give you free or "like free" life insurance. "Like free" means that the discount by adding it offsets the cost of it so you pay nothing more so you may as well add it.

~Investments~

Brokerage firms help you invest money. Typical investments include but are no where near limited to: Stocks, Bonds, Mutual Funds, CD's bought from multiple banks, and more.

~Credit and Lending~

Lending is the true purpose of any bank. To use someone else's money to lend to you and make you pay the bank and the other person for it. Loans, Lines of Credit, and Credit Cards are the primary vehicles by which they lend the money out. But the details can vary wildly within those categories.

~Key~

Remember our case study: Robert? He learned a small but powerful key to living in financial success. That key was doing things right, conservatively, and taking time to research decisions. He learned over time the various products the banks offered and used them to his advantage.

They key to using a bank to your advantage is taking the time to understand the products available and compare products between banks and within a bank. Make informed wise decisions. Don't go ahead with anything until you've taken the time to understand what you are doing. On the other hand, once you have decided on a course of action go forward with it. Each step toward your goals will lead you to another step. The journey of 1,000 miles begins with a single step.

Section II

Products

$

4

CHECKING

I know I can't be the only person who thought this… but prior to my very first day working for a bank I had no idea there was more than one type of checking account. I figured a checking was a checking and a savings was a savings. I never thought of them as "products".

The checking account is a bit of a misnomer these days. Most people don't write checks. In fact, for good reasons, check writing is becoming a thing of the past. As it started a checking account was created as a place to store your money so that you could safely go about not having to carry loads of cash. Then you could write a "check" which was a paper promising those funds to another person or company.

~History~

Fact Monster[7] Provides an interesting brief history here is an excerpt:

"According to most history texts, it probably wasn't until the early 1500s, in Holland, that the check first got widespread usage. Amsterdam in the sixteenth century was a major international shipping and trading center. People who had accumulated cash began depositing it with Dutch "cashiers," for a fee, as a safer alternative to keeping the money at home. Eventually the cashiers agreed to pay their depositors' debts out of the money in each account, based on the depositor's written order or "note" to do so."

~Recent Times~

People used checks as the primary non cash payment method up until the 1970's when ATM's became widespread. The use of credit cards and debit cards didn't really take on as the preferred payment method until after the 1990's really got underway. Many people from older generations are still without computers or cards, but banks around the world debate even accepting checks in the future. The burden of processing a check and recovering from potential fraud are higher than ANY other type of

---

[7] http://www.factmonster.com/ipka/A0001522.html

payment method. Just think how easy it is to order a new card VS getting a new account number and re setting up direct deposits etc.

~Interesting Facts~

The following was copied from ehow.com[8]:

"1971 - First true bank ATMs: Docutel introduces its Total Teller, the first true fully functioning bank ATM.

1978 - The first IBM-compatible Diebold machine is installed at a bank in Indianapolis.

The Expansion of Card Usage

Although the usage of the debit card at the POS has not surpassed the credit card as the preferred card medium of exchange, it has made tremendous strides in its commonality. A paper written by Robert M. Hunt of the Federal Reserve of Philadelphia notes that from 1980 to 2000, consumer purchases via debit card rose from zero percent to 12 percent, and purchases made via check fell from 86 percent to 50 percent.

Future Implications

If the recent move by British banks is any indication, the use of debit cards will skyrocket over in the next 10 years. Banks in Great Britain have agreed to stop accepting checks by 2018. They note factors such as the high relative cost of processing checks, coupled with the decline in merchants that accept checks as payment. "

---

[8] http://www.ehow.com/about_6192272_history-atm-card.html

~Now~

It's interesting that they noted that checks will not be accepted in Great Britain by 2018. Although there is no such plan in the United States, it does underscore the growing trend away from checks and toward debit cards as the preferred method of direct payment.

These days the check is not the preferred payment method of most institutions. Due to a new law called Check-21[9] many companies are now clearing checks electronically anyway to avoid the hassles. Have you ever tried to write a check at a store and the cashier ran it through then handed it back to you? Thanks to check 21 getting your "Canceled Checks" or even "Check Images" are becoming more and more unlikely. Those who need good records for tax reporting are now best off using the bank provided online bill payment services for the safest and best record keeping.

~My Account~

There are many checking account types offered by banks all going by different names. But here are the basics and categories:

---

[9]   http://en.wikipedia.org/wiki/Check_21_Act

All checking accounts at their most base level are for unlimited use of your money. You put money in and then use it as you need it, whether that is to make a purchase or pay a bill. The difference between accounts comes from what restrictions or privileges you get. Some accounts offer free check orders, free bill payment services, even a small interest rate. Other benefits may include a discount on services such as transfers to other banks or countries, waived stop payment fees, waived Non Bank ATM fees, and more. Sometimes the bank may give you an interest rate discount on a loan or a bonus on a CD. Some banks honor their higher value clients with discounts on brokerage trades. You could find you get a better insurance rate by having a long history and relationship with a specific bank. You may find a loan easier to get by having a history with the bank you are applying through.

There can be packages and accounts available for Students, Military Members, and Employees of Member Companies, The Elderly or retirees may have accounts with privilege. Those with lots of money almost always have special accounts available.

~Value~

Why do people with more money get more? The fact is, despite all the talk about fees and overdrafts in recent times, banks make over 80% of their profit from less than 20% of their clients. The wealthier the client the more money they bring in profit for the bank. These are the clients taking big loans and making big deals and keeping the most in the bank to loan to others. Rightly, the bank provides special things for people who bring this important business. Hopefully that helps take out some of the wonder about checking accounts.

$

5

SAVINGS

In addition to checking accounts the banks offer savings accounts. This is where you keep money that you may need within 6 months or less, but probably won't need within 30 days. There are two primary purposes to having a savings.

1. To keep money out of your checking so that you are less likely to spend it.

2. To have a place to add to your savings and build it up. Investment advisers say you should have 6-9 months income in your savings at any one time.

Generally speaking a savings account with no restrictions will pay less interest. Some savings accounts pay a higher rate of return in exchange for time commitment. These savings accounts are known as "CD's (certificates of deposit)" or "Time accounts". A normal savings may be paying 0.15% for $5,000 while a CD may pay 5% for the same $5000 for committing to leave it in for 6 to 12 months. "I don't want to lock away my money… what if an emergency comes up?" That is a great question. I have a question for you first. "What if you have no emergency how much money will you loose after three years of waiting for an emergency?" Any funds you don't plan on needing for 6 months or more should be placed in CD's if the rates are much higher. Some people use the emergency excuse for not putting money into a CD. For example they'll say that if an emergency came up like car repairs, or doctors bills that they didn't plan on or expect and they need the money they don't want to have to pay the interest penalties for taking it out. This could sound reasonable. But it's usually not.

The money is there for emergencies. That's one of the many reasons to own a savings account is to put money away for a time you may need it or want it. These are not good reasons, however, to stay out of CD's unless the emergency you're referring to is not unexpected. If you're actively looking for a house and expect to buy soon, or you have a relative who is sick and likely to need medical expenses paid then maybe you were wise to withhold from a CD. Possible emergencies that you don't even know about are not good reasons to avoid putting money into a CD. Leave some out for emergencies and put some in for interest. Leave out 40% and put in 60%. Think strategically.

~Thinking Beyond Today~

If you need to take the money out early for some unseen emergency you will typically still earn more on the money long term even after the small penalty they charge to take it early. It's wise to put it in because if you put it in for a one year term but then had to break it out after 8 months and paid a 6 month interest penalty, you still earned two months of good interest and that was probably more than you would have earned in a year in the lower interest savings account.

If you didn't end up needing it you were even wiser because now you haven't lost those other 6 months of interest. You remember our case study Robert? He only put $2,000 in of his own money and never touched it. Where did the $48,000 come from? Compounding. Compounding is one of the most powerful forces in the world of finance.

~Exercise: Math Time~

The money earned in a Savings/CD or for that matter the interest you pay on a loan is calculated by most banks using a formula called daily compounding. This is the formula to compute compounded interest for one month:

(BALANCE) X (RATE) X (DAYS IN STATEMENT CYCLE)

(365)

Robert put in $2,000 of his own money. In order to calculate this we must know how to turn a percentage into a decimal figure. To do this simply take the decimal point and move it two spaces to the left. For example 10 % is the number 10.00. Then move the point to the left two spaces which is now 0.10.

As for statement cycles, most statement cycles will vary between 28-36 days. Short months, such as February will be less, and long months that include more weekends and holidays may be longer. However for our purposes we will use an average. The average month is 30 days. There are 365 days in a year.

~Example of Roberts IRA~
($2,000 X 0.10 X 30)÷365 = $16.44 Per Month

Robert only earned $16.44 the first month. If you took this amount times 12 months you get $197.28 for the first Year. If you then take that and multiply it by 18 years you only get $3,551.04. At a linear rate of growth he would have only earned $3,551.04 for 18 years worth of investment. So where did the growth come from? How did Robert gain over $48,000? That is where compounding comes in to play. The first month he earned $16.44. The next month his balance was $2016.44. So now you plug the new balance into the same equation and you get $16.57.

($2016.44 X 0.10 X 30)÷365 = $16.57

So the second month he's already earning more than the first month. As this process rolls on and on over the months and years the amounts will eventually get exponentially larger. The bottom line of compounding is: Your interest earns interest. This is one way to make your money work for you.

I once read a case study of a man who had saved over $850,000. He would take $45,000 a year to live on and keep the rest in a CD. However he was earning nearly $48,000 a year in interest. This means that after taking out his 45K he was still 3K ahead of the previous balance.

Every year his account would get bigger and his income would stay the same. This became a perpetual flow of income for him. This would only work as long as you had the right rate. As rates rise and fall he would have years where he did not earn more than he took out.

However, he also had years where he earned far more than what he took out. He found the best way to balance the flow was to lock in longer terms when he felt rates were peaking and about to drop again.

It's better for your money to work for you than for you to work for your money. This man had put his money to work and therefore he didn't have to work for his money. Also the $45,000 a year went much further because he owned both of his homes and all his cars debt free. The average person spends between one quarter and one third of their income on housing/mortgage/rent costs. If you didn't have to spend that money monthly you could be freed up to do a great many other things.

~Freedom~

What do you pay in mortgage or rent each month? What would you be able to do if you made the SAME income you do now, but DID NOT have to pay that amount to anything but yourself? Would you live differently? What Ministries could you give to? And that is exactly what your goal should be!!!!

$

6

INVESTMENTS

In addition to Savings and CD's, financial institutions also offer investment products. There are 3 basic products investment firms offer. There are many more products than these, however these are the three most common types. Other investment products usually take more experience and money. There are many books written on these, and as I am not a licensed investment specialist, I will sum up the basics. If you find this area interesting I encourage you to look into it more on your own. I would start by reading anything by Dave Ramsey[10]. The 3 basic areas are stocks, bonds, and mutual funds.

~Stocks~

Stocks are partial ownership in a company. You earn money two ways:

A. The company pays you when it makes profit; this pay is called a dividend. This could be higher or lower than standard interest.

---

[10] http://www.daveramsey.com

B. You can sell stocks at a price higher than you paid for them. You buy a share at $6 and sell at $8 you make $2.

The more shares you buy the more dividends are paid to you and the more you make when selling them. Stocks are the more risky investment because you can also buy a share for $20 and see the value drop to $6. You only really loose money if the company goes out of business or if you sell your shares when the value of your shares is low. Otherwise, if you wait long enough the value will go back up eventually, as long as it is a good company.

~Bonds~

Bonds are loans. Basically you lend money to companies (or the government) and the company (or government) pays you back plus interest.

It's like you become the bank. The longer the bond is kept the more you earn. The bonds risk is limited by the ability of the institution to pay you back. You can buy from the Federal Government, State Governments, even private companies. Obviously a relatively shaky company is much more risky then the federal or state government when it comes to the ability of that bond to be payed back to you.

~Mutual Funds~

Mutual Funds are a combination of investments. These make the most sense for most people. A mutual fund is where an investor buys many products which vary in type and degree of risk. The funds advisor then sells a share of that group of products. This is called a Mutual Fund. These funds may include CD's, Stocks, Bonds, and other products. There are different risk levels and therefore some are more stable while other have higher return potential.

~Starting Out~

These products and much more are offered through investment firms. The easiest way to get started investing is to either meet with an advisor, also known as a consultant, or do some research and start trading on your own.

You could meet with a financial consultant to review your opportunities. A meeting with an advisor usually requires that you have at least $500 – $1000 that you are willing, even if not yet committed, to invest, but not always.

Another way to start your investing would be to open an online trading account and play with stocks on your own. If you're just starting out you could buy one or two shares at a time, just to see where it goes. It's like playing a strategy game at that point. As you get used to how things work you can put more money into it. I really enjoy penny stocks (Stocks Valued for less than $1 per share). It's an easy way to put just a few dollars, $10-$20, into the market and watch it grow or shrink without really risking anything important.

~Playing it Safe~

You should always keep in mind that the money you invest in non-FDIC products can loose value or even be lost. However, that money can also earn you a lot more returns than a simple savings account. Use money you are willing to loose. This sounds like a silly thing to say. Why would I want to loose money? It is a silly thing to say. Then again you spend money on games, TV, Movies or other entertainment without any monetary return all the time. You do this because there is a return of enjoyment. Consider this your entertainment money. So you aren't loosing money you are spending it. I say anything I would spend on disposable products can also be trading money. If you can spend $25, $100, or even a $1000 to eat or watch movies or go on trips then you can spend it to trade.

Especially when you're first starting out consider trading money as your excess money. Don't use the money that you've saved to live on or that 6-9 month income money. You can, however, budget in trading money to your savings plan, just like you budget in play money. By taking a few dollars here or there and putting them aside to trade you can start playing with the market while you're building your savings.

Again this should only be money your willing to spend, just as if you had bought food or fun with it. Consider playing the market like playing an arcade game. You may win coins back, or it may eat your coins. It can be fun even just to buy one share to watch and track it. No emotional based decisions here. You buy shares based on good research and a lot of prayer.

The good news is that investment firms can often help you with more secure products if you're not ready for the market yet. Many can help you buy FDIC and non-FDIC CD's, called "brokered CD's". They either base these CD's on various market factors or buy them from other banks.

By buying FDIC CD's through investment firms you can often obtain better rates of return than just using the bank down the street. The investment firm researches the best rates at all banks large and small. By having them buy more CD's through several smaller banks you can spread your FDIC coverage. Since all are maintained and managed by one institution and one investment advisor, you have the benefit of more earning power without having to drive yourself to multiple institutions.

That is the quickest run down I can give you about investments. You can learn more with a little research, I recommend starting with any materials by Dave Ramsey.

Ultimately remember two points:

- Investments CAN loose money…

- Do not buy anything until you have prayed it through thoroughly! Make sure that God said: "Yes!"

*Given the changes occurring in the world today, it could also be wise to seek other things to invest in. Property, Gold, Silver, Farm/Produce production, and other things of tangible value. When the markets do someday collapse and the world goes through change having debt free commodities that are innately valuable, such as those in the barter days I spoke of in the beginning of this book, could be a great thing to have on hand. Gold and Silver, if just bought for value should be bought in bulk sizes. However if bought for the potential of trading in a pinch should be bought in small sizes such as 1/4 or even 1/8 of an ounce.

$

7

RETIREMENT

If you Fail to Plan… you are Planning to Fail. There are few things that are more overlooked in financial planning than retirement. I regularly talk to people in their 50's and 60's who have saved nothing for retirement. When asked when they will retire they all say they would like to retire between 65-70 years old. But what will they retire on? Social Security doesn't pay enough to fund a lifestyle. Given the state of Social Security it may not even be available much longer. I want to share some stories with you to get you thinking about your latter years.

~Planning Case Studies~

Let's take a look at some retirement case studies. Martha worked for a bank when they came out with a new product called an I.R.A (Individual Retirement Arrangement) (*See IRS Publication 590*)[11]. The name actually came from one of the men working on the project at Federal level, Ira Cohen. So she, like our earlier case study Robert, put $2k aside in an IRA. They guaranteed her 10%

---

[11] http://www.irs.gov/publications/p590/ar01.html#d0e295

on her money until she turned 60. This was her 60th birthday. She now had over \$65,000 in just that one account.

In the same city a few miles away lives an older woman named Rita. She was working at a local department store as a greeter until she broke her ankle at 71 years old. She lives alone. She lives on a "fixed income" which means that she doesn't work and receives only from her Social Security money. She only gets a fixed \$1,200 a month from SSI.

Martha lives in her home paid off and drives her debt free car. Rita lives in a small studio apartment in a rough neighborhood. So how did they end up like this? If you fail to plan you are planning to fail. Each woman made choices that lead her to her current state.

~Precaution Case Study~

It's not always a failure of planning and working, sometimes it's a failure of taking precautions. I once worked with a couple. They are in their 80's at the time. He says to me, "You know, I was once a great business man…we had so much money we could go anywhere, buy anything, drive any car. I had more money than you shake a stick at."

I asked him "what happened?" As he stands here telling me his story with an un-ending grin he and his wife are handing out samples at a grocery store.

"Well", he says "I made a bad business deal…actually the business deal was great, but the guy I was partners with used it to take everything and leave me to fall for it. We lost everything in the after math, even the house. If I'd just taken a couple of extra steps I could have put safe guards in place and prevented either the whole thing from happening or the effects of it from hitting so hard. But I like people and I trusted him and I was blinded by how much money I was going to make on it.

~Planning Ahead~

These days you cannot count on social security even being available for you when you retire. Many times people don't stay with one company for 30 years in order to get a pension plan, which are not commonly offered anymore anyway. So how do you plan for the latter years? You can be sure of 2 things:

1). God will have to be your source. Money is a resource, jobs are a resource, investments can be a resource, but only God can be your source. Allow his ways and His wisdom and His Word to be your light!

2). You must plan. If you fail to plan; you plan to fail. Allow the leadership of the Holy Spirit through prayer to give you divine instructions and plans. God was speaking to everyone in 2007 to get out of the stock market before it crashed. Those who listened to him got out, those who didn't got stuck right in the middle of it. You don't just plan, you pray through His plan for your life. So what kinds of things do financial institutions offer that you can participate in?

~401K~

Most companies offer a retirement account, plan or service. When you meet whatever guidelines and requirements the company offers you can start to have money taken out of your paycheck and put into one of these retirement vehicles. You can have what you put in matched by your employer.

For example you put in $50, your company puts in $50.This means that by adding $50 to your 401k you actually added $100. What makes this even better is the $50 is before taxes. So if you made $2,000 gross income (before taxes) then you actually only get taxed on $1,950.00. This can mean less going to taxes and in some cases can mean you pay so much less toward taxes that your actual Net (money after tax) paycheck is the same, or slightly less. Really if your employer matches your contribution (which means that if you put in $50 they put in another $50 so now you have $100) some people would tell you that you are literally throwing away money by not putting at least as much as they will match in the plan. The beauty of these types of plans is that they are automatic. There is no thinking or discipline, it just goes away and you forget it's there.

Many people don't build enough savings. They focus on more immediate needs. Another benefit to the 401K is that you build a forced savings from which you can pull from in an emergency. If you need the money you can borrow from your 401K. It acts as a loan with interest but the money you pay back through payroll deductions all goes into your 401K, including the interest. You borrow from yourself and pay yourself back plus some. Sometimes you can withdraw the money without borrowing it. If you did it would get a penalty tax taken from the amount you withdrew, usually about 20% goes to penalty tax if you withdraw the funds before you turn 59 ½ years old. You may say why have a 401K if you can't take money out without penalties? Most people don't save so they would have zero to borrow from without this. Another factor to consider is that many times half of that money was put in by your employer if they do matching, so really the employer is paying your 20% tax. 80% of $2,000.00 which you saved is better than 100% of $0.00 that you didn't save.

Another great thing about 401K plans is that if you move companies before you retire (which my statistics show you are more likely to do these days) then you can take it with you. This was not true as much with many pensions.

The down side of these plans is that you are limited to the small group of investments that the 401K plan administrator offers. They may not give you any FDIC insured products or any access to annuities. If you want better or broader choices, and you are willing to put some away each month without them making you through payroll deductions, you could be better off with other products.

~IRA~

So what if you decided to open your own business or work for a smaller business that has no retirement plan? What if you want other options not included in a 401K? Or what if you wanted better access to the money should you need it? An IRA is an Individual Retirement Arrangement. These accounts are self directed, which means that you are in charge of getting money in and you are in charge of making sure you keep on top of that money so it grows as you wanted it to. If your company does not offer matching to your 401K this could be a better place to put your retirement. The draw backs are that it is not payroll deducted so you have to remember to put it in and report it on the taxes, and that you can make higher dollar contributions to the 401K. The benefits are that the money is more accessible, should you need it, and that you have greater control over what it is invested in, even an FDIC insured Savings or CD if you like, which many if not most 401K's do not have.

IRA's can be in nearly any vehicle. Which means you can put your money into CD's and savings accounts or you can invest your money in the market with investments. You can even have gold and silver purchasing plans through an IRA. As long as that company slaps the IRA label on it, nearly any product type could be an IRA. Check with your bank or financial institution about what IRA products they offer. Look also for alternative programs, but make sure to check any company through the better business bureau at www.bbb.org.

In order to understand IRA's you must see them as having two parts. There is an IRS side and a Bank side. Understanding The IRS side of IRA and the Bank side of

IRA can be confusing. But let's make it simple. Think of the IRS term "IRA" as the umbrella, or the label. Think of the Bank side as the container. You can place the "IRA" label on many containers and they will all conform to the IRS rules AND the rules of that container. There are several types of IRA's but they are all just labels.

Example:

"IRA"	BANK
Traditional	Savings
Roth	CD/Time Account
SEP	Investment Account
ESA	

You can have an IRA savings or an IRA brokerage. If you have an IRA savings it will still function as a savings would, earning interest. The IRA savings will simply have the additional functions of an IRA which means that the interest you earn will not be included on your taxes until you take it out, or possibly never.

~IRA Types~

IRA's come in several forms. The two that you are most likely to use and see are the Traditional and ROTH. In short, the SIMPLE and SEP IRA's are for small employers and self employed people. If you are in that situation these may be something you want to do research on. Often self employed individuals and business owners can make contributions (deposits) into a SIMPLE IRA on behalf of themselves and on behalf of the company they own. This gives the individual tax benefits and the company also gets tax benefits. You can also place money into a SEP IRA for your employees, also getting a business tax write off.

An ESA is an Education Savings Account. This is an IRA designed to build a savings for education expenses of a child. You can get a tax deduction for putting money into a savings for your child and the child can then take out the money tax free and use it for school later in life.

~Traditional IRA~

The two IRA types we will focus on here are the Traditional and ROTH. The traditional IRA is the most basic form and it is the most used. It is similar to a 401k in that you put money into the retirement account in order to reduce your taxable income. But your employer does not add to this plan. And you can put in less per year then a 401k. Typically the IRA has a limit of $5000 per year in contributions versus contributions as high as 25% of your income in a 401K. The limits are higher for those over 50 and change from year to year. However unlike the 401k where they handle the money for you, in an IRA you are in charge of your money. This is bad if you neglect it because no one is watching it to help it grow for you but great if you're on top of the account because who's more motivated than you to do right by your money.

To give you an idea of how this works let's look at an example. If you make $40,000 gross (pretax) income, and you place $5,000 into a Traditional IRA, you will be taxed on $35,000 gross income. The amount of money you pay in taxes will be less. Let's say that you are using a tax service, such as TaxAct.com or TurboTax.com, and the calculator came out with a result of owing the government $500 in taxes. If you go back and tell the system that you contributed $2000 into a Traditional IRA you may be surprised to see that you are now getting a $1500 refund.

How did you go from owing $500 to getting a refund of $1500? You reduced your taxable income and less became owed. If you already have money set aside for something at tax time you may find placing that into a Traditional IRA for your later years will cause you to get money back from the IRS.

Not only can Traditional IRA's reduce your taxable income in your working years, but for many people income is lower in retirement years. This means that when you take out the money in your retirement years the money will be taxed at a lower rate, because the IRS taxes you at different rates depending on income levels. If you are very wealthy in your older years it will be taxed at a higher rate, however being wealthy it doesn't hurt as much as it would in your developing years. Either way the Traditional IRA has benefits for your income today as you are putting money in.

The IRS wants you to save for retirement, so there are penalties for taking money out before 59 ½ years old. The IRS will take 10% of any money you take out early, unless it is for one of the few exception reasons they list. These exceptions can be found in IRS Publication 590. However because the IRS wants their taxes they also have rules that require you take it out eventually. At 70 ½ years old you must start to take out from your IRA so that the government can take their taxes. Because you must start taking money out at 70 ½ you must also stop putting money in at this age as well.

~ROTH IRA~

A ROTH IRA is slightly different. This is for after tax money you put in. If you will be making more money or living at higher tax brackets in your retirement years, you may want to consider a ROTH IRA. The money you put in is AFTER TAX which means it will NOT reduce our taxable income up front. However all the money you earn on your money will typically grow tax free (consult a tax advisor).

If you recall Robert who put in $2000 and it grew to $48,000. If that was a Traditional IRA he would be taxed on all that growth. In a ROTH IRA that would tax free growth. Therein is the benefit. You don't get a break for putting money in, but you get tax sheltered or tax free growth. The IRS doesn't care how long you keep the money in a ROTH IRA because it's after tax money anyway. Since the IRS is not going to get paid from the money anyway you can continue putting money in to grow tax free well beyond the 70 ½ limit placed on traditional IRA's.

~Annuities~

Annuities are products sold through insurance companies. These can be complicated but a very elementary understanding would be that you buy the policy from the company at one value and agree to let it mature with them for some time. At the maturity you can either redeem the policy for the increased value or take monthly payments. If you choose monthly payments they could go on and on for the rest of your life, even paying you more than the value of the annuity plan. The payments, if this was your arrangement could continue until the company goes out of business or you die. There are terms and conditions and some companies are stronger than others.

~Summary~

The 401K is an employer plan, managed by, primarily the employer. You can choose within the plan the investments you want, but only those that they offer. IRA's can give you the freedom to mange them on your own, or with advice.

If you leave your employer you will almost always want to take the 401K and role it into your new employers plan or into an IRA. If you do roll it into an IRA you can get to the money MUCH easier than you can when it is in the 401K.

As Robert's case study taught us, enough right decisions over a long enough time can create a successful plan of action. Here are a few thoughts to ponder. The journey to a thousand lands begins with a single step. Whether you're 15 and just starting to think about your money, or 50 and trying to catch up on a life passing you by, or 80 and on what you "think" is a "fixed" income. Small steps of wisdom can take you so much farther than you think. The seed you sow will take you where you want to go.

All investments are a personal decision, many could lose value. Therefore pray through any decision and seek the help of a trustworthy godly financial advisor. Make sure that they are an independent advisor and not one working for a major bank or insurance company. Advisors employed by financial institutions are given quotas of products to sell. They are more interested in their bottom line than your benefit regardless of what they tell you. They have to be, that is what they are employed to do. An independent advisor, one not working on behalf of a specific financial institution, would be more likely to lay all available alternatives with the full pro's and con's for you.

$

8

ONLINE

Online has become a household word in only the last 20 years. Many people shy away from doing banking online because they fear "hacking" or fraud. This is a genuine but misguided concern. With every step hackers take to break down security, companies move two steps closer to protecting your security. Of all bank fraud less than 5% is committed using information obtained through electronic means.

While it is not easy to obtain information electronically, it is easy to obtain information physically and then use it electronically. Most people who are smart enough to use computers to hack in and obtain information without getting traced or caught would not waste time on getting into one persons $300,000.00 account. For that matter someone who had the sophistication to hack past electronic security would just as easily hit the banks main databases to get multiple sets of people's information, not one person's online account.

In fact keeping yourself off-line doesn't actually prevent anything. You don't have to do any online banking yourself to have your information taken from a bank computer database, which is the real target of most hackers. Banking online can add to your security much more than take away from it. Many banks have a 100% guarantee against fraudulent activity on your accounts accessed through any means anyway. If yours doesn't, I suggest moving banks.

~Online Security~

When doing anything online that involves releasing your personal or account information there are two important things to keep in mind. Only deal with known reputable companies and make sure that the page you are inputting your card information on has an S after the HTTP, like this: HTTPS://

If you are unsure of the company you can check the history of the company, such as, how long has it been open? Check the Better Business Bureau.[12] You can also do a search through a major search engine such as Google, Yahoo, or Bing. See if you find complaints or articles about them.

---

[12] http://www.bbb.org/

Just as importantly make sure you see "HTTP**S**"[13] at the top of your browser. The "S" makes a BIG difference.

HTTP://www.acompany.com

vs.

HTTPS://www.acompany.com

The 'S' stands for secure. An HTTPS website has taken certain precautions to be registered as a secure site with various authorities. What does HTTPS stand for? Hypertext Transfer Protocol over a Secure Socket Layer Without going into lots of computer lingo this means that there have been layers of registered codes and protection to keep your information from being received or used by anyone other than the company you intended on using. It doesn't mean EVERY page on the website has to have the "S" but at least the page that you enter your information on does.

~Online Services~

In addition to providing online access to view account balance and transactions most banks offer a variety of online accesses and services. Some of these services are: Spending reports that categorize spending; Budget tools; Bill Pay Services; Savings Plans; Electronic Statement

---

[13] http://en.wikipedia.org/wiki/HTTP_Secure

Delivery; Photocopies of Statements, Deposits, Checks; Personalized ATM/Debit and Credit Cards; and Access to loans and other bank products. Online Banking is the best way to run your accounts saving you time and keeping your account safer. The main thing to take away from this is that: Not using online does not prevent fraud and using online banking does not increase risk, it reduces it.

~Bill Pay~

The bank can pay your bills for you. When available the bank will pay bills electronically. When the company accepting the payment doesn't accept electronic payment most banks will send a cashier check on your behalf. Your party receiving their money is guaranteed funds and you stay safe by not having your account number on it and pay no postage. Some banks even take care of third party late fees if it's not received and many banks waive the stop payment fee if you use Bill Payment service and the item is not received. The main idea here is that you are sending the money to them without releasing your account number instead of having them take the money which opens the possibility for them to take the wrong amount on the wrong date, or take a payment that you didn't ask them to, or continue to draw payments you keep asking them to cancel. If they don't get your account number or card number they have no ability to hit your account at their will. Using Bill Pay keeps your account information out of their hands.

~Online Statements~

Online statements allows you the access to print your statements from your home computer or even view them online without printing. You can also save them to a PDF copy onto your hard drive or store that copy on a remote hard drive, such as Google Docs or Sky Drive. This prevents the statements from being lost in the mail or miss-delivered to your neighbor's house, or stolen from your mail. You can access statements, usually, for up to seven years online at most banks. You can even send copies at request to those requesting them when trying to get a house or apartment without touching paper. It makes record keeping safer with quicker access.

~Online Fraud DE-Mystified~

There is a lot of mystery and apprehension surrounding doing things online. I've decided to dedicate a section just to this topic to take away the mystery and help you navigate the waters. The fact is that doing your banking online is the safest way to do your banking, however purchasing online and Email are tricky matters.

For more information I suggest starting with some online articles by the FDIC. Go to FDIC.GOV and type in "Fraud Prevention Brochure" or type in the link at the bottom of this page[14].

Here is the bottom line for those who don't want all the details. Fraud online usually involves one of two things:

1. Someone tricks you into giving up your information.

2. Someone steals your information physically and then uses it online.

So what is the solution? Know who you are giving info to and don't use paper for people to get a hold of.

If you are truly concerned about security, you must realize that paper is not your friend. Do nothing by paper. Do not write checks, use the mail, have statements mailed to you, or otherwise conduct your affairs in paper. If someone can get a hold of it, they will. How then can I do anything? E-Statements not mail delivery. The same copy will be yours in less than half of the time and if you need paper records you may print it out yourself so you need no mail person to miss-deliver it. If you intend on keeping paper copies around the house after you printed your statements from online, keep them in a locked secure place.

---

[14] http://www.fdic.gov/consumers/theft/

Criminals, during home and office break-ins now search for information even more than for cash, gold or jewelry.

Here is some interesting data to consider. Checks account for most fraud loss and of complaints reporting a dollar loss the highest median losses were found among checks[15]. 75% of companies cited employees as a likely source of hacking attacks[16] (which means that not signing up for online has no preventative effect because the employees already have your information.) Banks in Great Britain have agreed to stop accepting checks as a payment method by 2018 citing security and cost as reasons[17] [18].

I hope this subdues some of your online stress. If not just realize that this is the direction of the world. What if all the computers in the world crash? The banks use the computers so your checks still won't be any good.

---

[15] http://www.consumerfraudreporting.org/internet_scam_statistics.htm

[16] http://www.3w.net/lan/internet-use-statistics.html

[17] http://www.ehow.com/about_6192272_history-atm-card.html

[18] http://www.npr.org/templates/story/story.php?storyId=121529285

Section III

Pitfalls

$

9

POSTING

There are many pitfalls to keeping a basic checking account. Understanding a few basics will put you light years ahead of the pack. Understanding posting order, cut off times, debit card tracking, and keeping a register are the most basic and yet least understood arenas in keeping a bank account.

First let's take a look at posting and cut off times. Banks receive items to process on accounts through many channels throughout the day. Some of these channels include the branch, ATM, phone customer service, online, and many other departments that deal directly with other banks or the Federal Reserve. For practical reasons there must be a time of day each channel gathers that days transactions and sends them off to processing.

~Cut Off Times~

The department that processes transactions is not at the branch but in a central location. They process the days work from all of the locations nearby. These folks work with the Federal Reserve and clearing houses beginning work at a pre determined point in the evening and work right on through the next morning, Monday night through Friday night. Usually their work from the night posts between 5-8 am the next morning.

If you've ever wondered why a deposit made Friday night or Saturday is not available on Monday it is because the first processing of the week isn't done until Monday night. Posting from the previous nights work is available the next morning. So Tuesday morning through Saturday morning deposits become available. For example deposits made before cut off on Friday post Saturday morning, deposits made after cut off Friday post Tuesday morning.

All banks work this way in some fashion or another because this is when the Federal Reserve does their processing. The Federal Reserve and Clearing House are the mediators between banks. Almost all transactions between banks pass through either the Federal Reserve or Clearing House or both.

Some banks that have gone nearly completely electronic are able to have no cut of times, because they are not physically sending anything to the processing center. However, most banks still have a daily cut off time of around 4pm. Sometimes, in a remote area furthest from a processing center, a branch may set a cut off time as early as 2pm. That means that if you make a deposit on

Wednesday at that remote branch at 2:30 pm it won't be sent for processing until Thursday night.

Typically this processing is done overnight and posts the next morning. So at that remote branch a deposit made at 2:30 pm on Wednesday afternoon won't be sent for possessing until Thursday afternoon and won't post and become available to you until Friday morning. This deposit will cover items processed to the account on Thursday because banks will post deposits before withdrawals; however it will not cover items processed on Wednesday night even though the deposit was made on Wednesday.

Check with your bank for their specific rules, make sure to read them in your disclosures and do not take a representatives word for it. Many base level employees don't understand it any better than you do.

Another important note, many processing channels are not related to customer interaction but deal directly with other banks. This means you may not see items that are waiting to be processed that day as "pending". ACH and Checks are the most common. They do not show as pending during the day, but the next morning you see them posted. When forgotten these may cause the account to become overdrawn.

For these items normally you will wake up on Thursday morning and see items processed Wednesday night even though they were not showing as pending all day Wednesday. The next day then, Thursday in this example, is when many banks view items that posted negative and decide what to pay and return. At that time they assess any overdraft or return fees. For you visual learners, let's look at this example on a register.

~Cut Off Example~

Your Record Ex 1

Your Record			
Date	Transaction	Amount	Balance
Monday	Open Account	X	X
Monday	Deposit	100	100
Monday	Check # 99	-60	40
Tuesday	Card Purchase 3pm	-3.5	36.5
Tuesday	Deposit 5pm	200	236.5
Tuesday	Check # 100 5:30pm	-120	116.5

According to your own record you have $116.50. However you failed to keep in mind that the cut off time at your bank is 4pm. You then gave someone a check at 5:30pm but their bank does electronic processing and is able to do same day processing and it hits your bank that night. So according to the bank it looks like this.

Banks Record Ex 1 Continued

Banks Record			
Date	Transaction	Amount	Balance
Monday	Open Account	X	X
Monday	Deposit	100	100
Monday	Check # 99	-60	40
Tuesday	Card Purchase 3pm	-3.5	36.5
Tuesday	Check # 100	-120	-83.5
Thursday AM	Overdraft Fee	-40	-123.5
Thursday PM	Deposit	200	76.5

Your Real balance is now $76.50

~Posting Order~

In July 2010 the federal government stepped in to regulate the banks. Now all states will follow the following rules, generally. They will always post any deposit scheduled for that nights processing first before withdrawals. Always post card transactions next. They will then post Checks, Bill Pays, ACH, Etc.

They may still post items highest amount first. They may still charge overdraft fees for each item that posts negative; however there are new limits on how many overdraft fees per day. They must decline any purchase using a card that doesn't have sufficient funds, unless the customer has opted in to allow overdraft approvals on the card.

This last part has been tricky. It does not mean that the banks are no longer charging overdrafts for card transactions. It simply means that if the money is not in the account it will be declined. For example if the balance available at the time you swipe your card is $10 you cannot make a purchase for $11. However, if you have $5 in your account and you go to the gas station, which will show at first as $1 until you pump and finish your gas, than it will be approved by the bank. If it then posts for more than $5 you will pay an overdraft fee, you are the only one who can know your balance. This issue is causing a lot of confusion for people. Many are thinking that banks are not charging overdraft fees any more and this is not true.

~Direct Deposit~

If you have direct deposit you normally get paid every Friday or other Friday. Your employer shoots your deposit through their bank, then to the Federal Reserve, and finally to your bank some time between Thursday evening and Friday morning. There is no "12 midnight" rule about this. It will come in when it comes in. Remember this is after the cut off time for any bank. Because the direct deposit is electronic the bank will usually add it to the balance available to you right away even though it hasn't actually gone through possessing or posted to the account. That means you can call and see a positive available balance on Friday morning but still receive fees later in the day for items that posted negative with Thursday nights processing. You see, although available, the direct deposit will not post to the account until its processed Friday night, which means Saturday morning. It does not cover Thursday nights items.

~Cut Off Example~

You wrote a rent check on Thursday night expecting it would take a few days to clear. But your apartment managers use a bank that does electronic processing and that check clears the same day you gave it to them.

Direct Deposit 9AM			
Date	Transaction	Amount	Balance
Monday	Open Account	X	X
Monday	Deposit	100	100
Thursday	Check # 605 Rent	-850	-750
Friday	Direct Deposit	1050	300

You wake up Friday morning and see your balance is $300 and you say "Oh, my rent check cleared good." But you don't consider that it cleared to a negative balance.

Later that day the bank reviews the overdrafts and decides to pay the check but there is an overdraft fee.

Direct Deposit 1PM			
Date	Transaction	Amount	Balance
Monday	Open Account	X	X
Monday	Deposit	100	100
Thursday	Check # 605 Rent	-850	-750
Friday	Overdraft Fee	-40	-790
Friday	Direct Deposit	1050	260

You checked your balance at 9AM and went to the grocery store. You swiped your card as credit and paid for groceries totaling $200 from one store and $98 from another. So you figure you have $2 left in the account.

Direct Deposit Your Record			
Date	Transaction	Amount	Balance
Monday	Open Account	X	X
Monday	Deposit	100	100
Thursday	Check # 605 Rent	-850	-750
Friday	Direct Deposit	1050	300
Monday	Card Purchase	-200	100
Monday	Card Purchase	-98	2

However the bank charged a fee, so on Monday night that card purchase goes through and Tuesday morning you have another fee.

Direct Deposit Aftermath			
Date	Transaction	Amount	Balance
Monday	Open Account	X	X
Monday	Deposit	100	100
Thursday	Check # 605 Rent	-850	-750
Friday	Overdraft Fee	-40	-790
Friday	Direct Deposit	1050	260
Monday	Card Purchase	-200	60
Monday	Card Purchase	-98	-38
Tuesday	Overdraft Fee	-40	-78

You don't check your balance again until Thursday and now you are thinking how am I overdrawn by -$78? This is when you call the 800 number confused.

Typically banks charge a fee for each item that posts negative. Most banks post larger items first and smaller second. This results in more fees but less chance of big important items (like mortgage/rent/car payments) from being returned. The fees can be anywhere from $20-$70 per item. Those prices increase every year. For our example I used $40 as an average of what I've seen among the major banks.

*Note: a new process called "Date of Origination" posting is beginning to creep up. Some banks and states have begun using this already and the projection is that all banks will cross over to this new method. It began as an answer to those who complained that they did 10 purchases on a Saturday and a large Mortgage Payment came out on Monday and it posted first (because items are posted high to low) and caused more than one overdraft fee.

Therefore, many banks are now processing items by date and category. This makes things far more confusing. For example, you could do 10 purchases on Saturday and have a Mortgage payment come out Monday and the Saturday items post first and Monday's payment next and you only get one fee. But what if you did the 10 purchases on Saturday and you realized that would cause an overdraft and you wanted to cover it so you put in a deposit in Monday. The items from Saturday post first and the deposit Monday post next and you are still going to get fees from Saturday's overdraft. You cannot make a "catch up" deposit in Date of Origination posting. You absolutely have to make sure the money is in the account before you use it. This sounds like a no brainer to those who keep a good record. But there are a lot of people who are doing things in a manner that they are hoping to make a deposit to cover them before they post. This will no longer work in the new system. The states where this has been piloted have all seen an increase in overdrafts despite the fact that it was the American public who demanded it be this way. Watch out for this change in your bank and your state soon.

~Overdraft Protection~

Each bank offers overdraft protection. The details on this can differ dramatically. Ask your bank for their policies. For our purposes here I'll give you the basics. There are several types of overdraft protection. The main two forms of protection are either a savings account or credit line. In either case when you become overdrawn the bank takes money from your protection account and places that money into your checking account to cover the overdraft. That means if by the end of the processing you have a total balance of $-78 than they will pull that amount from your savings/credit line to cover it, usually costing a transfer fee of about $10-$20. It may also cause interest if it's from a credit line. It wouldn't matter then whether it were 20 items that posted negative or 1 because it's just pulling over enough to cover the total negative balance at the end of that nights processing. The transfer fee is usually small and better than multiple overdraft fees the bank could charge without it.

Direct Deposit With OD Protection			
Date	Transaction	Amount	Balance
Monday	Open Account	X	X
Monday	Deposit	100	100
Thursday	Check # 605 Rent	-850	-750

Friday	Overdraft Fee	-40	-790
Friday	Direct Deposit	1050	260
Monday	Card Purchase	-200	60
Monday	Card Purchase	-98	-38
Monday	Overdraft Protect	53	15
Tuesday	Overdraft Protect Fee	-15	0

Under the new 2010 regulations, if you have five items that post to the account negative the bank may still charge up to four overdraft fees for that, which is one per item but maxed at four. Or you could have this protection and pay one small fee; usually between $10-$20. So do the math: one $15 fee or four $40 fees. Overdraft protection is better. In the example above you would have paid $15 with overdraft protection or $40 without it. If you can't get overdraft protection we'll discuss some options for you in the chapter titled: "Help!"

$

10

CARDS

The use of debit cards can also be a source of overdrafts. If you go to the store and the machine asks you "Debit" or "Credit" you can use either one as long as your bank card has a Visa/MasterCard logo. If it does not have that logo you may only use "Debit". If you select "Debit" the machine will then ask for your pin number. If you select the "credit" option you will not need the pin. You only sign for the purchase or enter your zip code.

~Debit~

If you say "Debit" and use your PIN (Personal Identification Number) the machine will run that purchase request through a Point of Sale Network, (P.O.S.) The most common POS networks are STAR, Interlink, and Plus. These are the same Networks used to get money from an ATM machine. When you use the card as a POS transaction it will be sent to the bank the same business day in which it is done. This means it will show immediately as pending then post that business day. If done before the cut off time on Friday the transaction will be processed Friday night and post Saturday morning. If done on Friday after the cut off time it will go through possessing Monday night and post Tuesday morning.

~Credit~

If you say credit at that same machine and swipe that same debit card with the Visa/Mastercard logo, you will think you did the same thing. This time it asks for your signature and or zip code. This time the transaction will go through the Visa or Mastercard Network. This is different in a few ways.

Credit is similar in that the transaction will still "Pend" to your account[19]. The credit function of your card is also similar in that both types of transactions come directly from your account.

Important note: This is NOT a credit / charge card. When you use a charge card or a credit card you build a balance which you pay back later. And a debit card whether you use "Debit" or "Credit" still comes out of your Checking Account.

~Confusion~

When you use the credit key the merchant receives an authorization to use the card. Whatever the original amount authorized is, will show as pending to the account. At a grocery store the amount will usually pend correct

---

[19] Reflected in available balance but not yet processed.

because the amount authorized was your final amount unless you realize after the card was swiped that there was a problem with the amount. However if the amount was wrong (or you authorized it for an amount other than the final amount) than the amount showing as pending will be wrong, it will be the first amount swiped.

Restaurants and Gas stations often pend for wrong amounts, such as for $1 or 20% over your bill. Online or Catalog orders will often show as pending the day of the order, fall off, and then post once the item ships, which can be months later if it is back ordered. Some smaller merchants don't batch daily or get backed up and may not catch a missed receipt for some time. Merchant or machine errors may cause items to pend two or three at a time, usually this corrects it self within a few days. Rental car companies will authorize a deposit which will pend and disappear. These are just a few of the more common reasons your card transactions can be just as hard to track as checks.

~Summary~

These are some examples of the many reasons pending amounts will be different than the final purchase. Also sometimes a problem with a purchase will cause more than one of the same amount from the same store to pend.

These authorizations will typically show as pending for 3-5 business days before posting for the correct amount. Sometimes when more than one of the same transactions pend, one will post and the others will still pend then disappear a few days later. This is because the merchant must submit an intention to finalize before the item can post. If the card was swiped and you then canceled the transaction or voided it than it will still show as pending to your account for 3-5 business days unless that merchant calls and releases the transaction. If the item is right but the merchant is slow to submit the intention to finalize the transaction may show as pending in your balance, disappear after 3-5 business days, and then be added back to your balance and post 2 weeks, 2 months, or a year later. This is why you keep every receipt and write every transaction in your register. You cannot know what hasn't posted without a written record.

These are problems only when you are calling to check balances and assuming that the balance you hear is your correct balance. This is not always true. People who write checks are used to understanding that checks may be outstanding and if they call for the balance they have to account for checks that have been written and not cleared.

People who are younger and don't write checks aren't so used to the concept, but they should be. The balance in your register is the only balance you should ever trust. When you call or go online or check the balance at the ATM, you are not getting your real balance. That balance doesn't mean anything to you unless you understand how it relates to the transactions that have and have not yet cleared. The reason you check with the bank is not to check a balance but to check and see which items have cleared and posted and which items have not. This allows you to update your register.

$

11

REGISTER

If you are not one to understand detailed facts let me just head off all I'm about to say with one simple rule to avoid overdrafts for the rest of your life. The bottom line is this: keep a separate written record and don't spend more than you have. Now for those who need more let's take a deeper look at that statement.

~Record~

A separate written record is one in which you write everything down from the largest payment to the smallest cup of soda. Using your online banking, as great a tool as it is does not excuse you from keeping a record separate from the bank. You can use paper and pen, or a software program like Quicken, or even build your own excel sheet. If you do use Quicken I don't advise downloading your history, input all the data manually. Downloading data can make it harder to catch fraudulent transactions. More than one person has called their bank about a small transaction only to find out it's been coming out for two years or more without their knowledge.

However you do it, you must track the transactions going in and out of your account separate from the bank. This is the only way to know for sure that no fraud is going on and find out what your balance is. The bank doesn't know your balance. There are many reasons why your real balance may not be the same as the balance showing online. Online (or at the ATM, 800 Number, or any other bank record) only reflects that which the bank has received not everything you have done. Even card transactions do not always come through right away. I actually heard someone once say totally serious: "How could I be overdrawn? I still have checks." This is a humorous but true example of a total lack of understanding how money and math works. This person should not have a bank account, or even handle money. They should have someone take care of things for them.

~How?~

Keeping a record does take work. One of the first things you must understand; just because you deposit a check into the bank doesn't mean it's available to use. Checks usually have to post to the account before you can use them. Also, checks may have holds placed on them, or even be returned as no good. If you have any doubt that the check you put in is good, wait a full three weeks before using the funds. That is how long it can take for a bank to find out that the check was no good (Yes even in 2011). That being said the first step, assuming that you start with a zero balance, is to input your deposits. You should not spend what you do not have.

~Available Balance~

What is my ledger balance VS my available balance?

When items post the result is a balance of some kind. This is called your "Ledger Balance" also known as your balance as of the last business day. It is the ending balance including everything that has officially posted but not the balance including any pending transactions (those that have not yet posted).

Your available balance is the Ledger Balance adding/subtracting anything showing as pending. As we said with checks there are instances where a deposit that is pending is not part of the available balance either. Unless the deposit was electronic it won't usually be available until it has posted. There are also lots of ways for your card transactions to not always show as pending all the time. Sometimes transactions especially card transactions may double or triple pend, pend for wrong amounts (more or less), pend for several days, then disappear and post at a later date.

Therefore always check your balance on a separate written record where you write everything down and add and subtract as you go. Not only is this a good idea, you are required to according to the bank in your disclosures. Calling for your balance, going online, ATM, or in any other way contacting your bank for your balance is not a replacement for a written record. If you contact the bank for your balance assume it's wrong!

Always look to your own records for up to date information. If you don't know your balance without contacting the bank, than no-one does especially the bank.

~Fees~

Overdraft fees are awful, high, outrageous, expensive, and... well you get the point. You know they are awful. I once had one item go through my account and cause several items to post into overdraft causing, more items to post into a negative balance and so forth. I paid over $450 just in fees that one month. I don't know about you, but I didn't have $450 to spend on fees, so it put me behind months.

Do you know who was to blame for that overdraft causing $450 in fees though? The Bank? The President?

The Congress? No. It was me. I set up the payment and agreed to have it auto deducted. I failed to account for it in my balancing. I did it, knowing full well the fees that could come if the balance was not there for it when it came. Therefore I am the only person to blame. The sooner you get a hold of that reality the sooner you can take action to prevent another fee on your account.

~Winds of Change~

On July 21st of 2010 a banking regulation was singed into law by president Obama. It is called the Dodd-Frank Wall Street Reform and Consumer Protection Act[20]. Immediately following this acts' passing banks were limited to how many overdraft fees could be charged per day and how they could approve and post items that could cause fees. Each bank drafted new policies around this regulation. Those two changes were only the beginning. As of the beginning of 2011 there are still 900 laws that still haven't been written from the stipulations of that act. The financial picture is changing. Banks are being restricted and so are the free services. What does this mean to you and your overdrafts? It may be a small bit harder to get a fee, but a great deal harder to ask the bank to reverse it.

---

[20] http://en.wikipedia.org

~Accounting 101~

The only sure fire way to avoid an overdraft fee is… drum roll please… to not overdraw. I know, magic right? Allow me to review accounting 101. Anyone can do this.

The correct way to use your account is to make a deposit (or add money) to your account. Then make withdrawals less than or equal to the amount deposited including any fees or charges.

Your Record			
Date	Transaction	Amount	Balance
Monday	Open Account	X	X
Monday	Deposit	100	100
Monday	Check # 99	-60	40
Tuesday	Card Purchase 3pm	-3.5	36.5

So now the balance is $36.50. However in the real world most people don't do things the way they are supposed to. The banks post items according to regulations. Your bank isn't making these rules, people in the Federal and State Governments are. Even different states may do things differently. Generally what happens is someone gets to the point above and then writes a check on Thursday expecting that the check won't come through until the direct deposit comes in Friday.

Usually this works but since companies have so many convenient electronic ways of clearing checks it could come in on Thursday.

Your Record			
Date	Transaction	Amount	Balance
Monday	Open Account	X	X
Monday	Deposit	100	100
Monday	Check # 99	-60	40
Tuesday	Card Purchase 3pm	-3.5	36.5
Thursday	Check # 100	-120	-83.5
Friday	Overdraft Fee	-40	-123.5
Friday	Direct Deposit	200	76.5

This causes an overdraft. Some banks can take your check, and clear your other bank on the same day. So you now understand how this happens. What if you are already in the middle of this? What if you are overdrawn so often you can't see how to get out of the cycle? What do you do now if you are overdrawn right now? Turn to the next chapter for help.

$

12

HELP!

Some people can separate and compartmentalize their finances easily. Some have no idea what they pay each month. Others are 6 months behind before they know how late they really are. You don't have to be strict to budgets but you do have to have guidelines and principles you live by. If you are behind, or you feel lost in financial windfall, don't worry you are not alone.

Many people who have long degrees after their name get lost when dealing with money. It's among the most important practical skills most people could learn, but many don't know where to start. We will examine a few things you can try if you are buried and don't know how to get out. Nothing comes fast and easy, but with some good information and willingness to try new things you can start your journey to a better place, one step at a time.

~Do Over~

If you find your life in chaos and you can't tell where your money is or is not going then you may want to start by starting over. Calling it a do over is just fine. In fact, if you have an account that is often overdrawn, you may even want to consider closing it and starting a new account number so that you can start your new register skills at square one. In addition, if there were automatic payments causing the overdrafts they will cease because that account is closed and they will not have your new account number. Don't give it to them either. Pay them in cash, with online bill pay, or money orders. If you deal often with overdrafts you should not give your card or account number to any merchants for payments, even one-time payments. Often they will start drafting automatically again once they have your new information, even if you told them not to. Don't put yourself in that situation. If they demand auto pay, set up a new account number separately just for auto pays and another for your main bills and spending.

~Cash Method~

The easiest budget is to take out cash, envelopes, and an inexpensive notebook. On each envelope write a category (gas, rent, groceries, bills, etc...). You can even keep a separate envelope for each bill. For each envelope you will have a separate notebook or section of a notebook. Some people even write their balances straight on the envelope and subtract as they go right on the envelope itself. Whatever works for you is the best way. Try it different ways until you find what works.

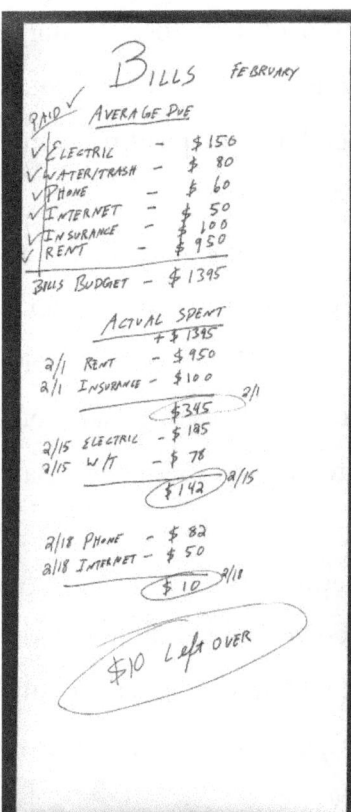

Tag each notebook section or envelope with a separate label and write on the first page the name of the category and balance (amount in envelope). In this example you will see "Bills" on the envelope. The deductions are taken each day. This person turned those cash deductions either into money orders, or made payments at local stores. In many cases you can pay an electric bill at the local grocery store customer service desk, or other partner business. Each time you make a withdrawal from the envelope you write down the date and amount and reason. As you get comfortable with this cash method you can eventually combine the envelopes of various catagories into one envelope. Then have one notebook for your cash. Then mark in that notebook the date, money, and category and in the separate category notebook you write the date, money, reason (specific).

This whole process isn't necessary forever, only until you have a firm, comfortable, grasp on where your money is going and you are disciplined to spend the right amount at the right places.

You should plan your monthly budget out to include everything from bills to fun. If you don't plan in the fun, you will do it anyway. You must plan fun or you will binge-spend causing more money to go to that than you would want which would take away from the money that should go to other things.

~Account Method~

Once you really get this down your ready to put all that money into an account. Start with money orders or Bill Pay and don't use an ATM/Check Card until you're thoroughly sure that you are ready.

Piece by piece you add services the bank offers. Stay away from credit cards unless and until you can honestly call yourself disciplined. Once you're sure you can use a credit card to your advantage, you could pay everything with the credit card and get one with a great rewards program. Make sure to pay it off in full every month never carry a balance on a credit card. They may offer amazing deals with 0% APR for 6 months. But what you don't know is that if the card isn't paid off within 6 months many companies will back date that interest to day one. Think of credit cards as a convenience tool, like a check or debit card. You don't use a credit card unless you have the money to pay it off. Credit cards can be useful because errors caused by merchants or fraud through use of the card won't affect your cash balances in your checking account directly, where as they will if you had used your debit card. Think of your debit card and credit cards as the same or similar tools.

~Separate Accounts~

I prefer having separate accounts for separate purposes. Much like an electronic version of the envelopes. I have one for just bills. Another for spending money. Another for tithe and offering. Another budgeted for the kids. You could also use one for business purposes, budgeting play money, gas money, or hobby money. Any time you need to allocate funds for a special purpose a separate account could be useful, as long as you keep track of what is what. I have my direct deposit split into each account automatically. Tithe then is as simple as going online and sending that payment from that account twice a month. I have a little extra put in there to save for special offerings or things God may want me to do for Him; such as buying someone a hamburger or a new car. I know my money is His, so I plan for Him to ask me for it's use to further His kingdom.

~Computer Method~

Quicken is among the most popular budgeting programs available. I strongly recommend using a computer based program to act as your electronic register. It helps ensure you are not making mathematical errors in the record keeping process. If all you have is pen, paper, and calculator you may forget where you left off, or hit the wrong button. If you miss tally the total and don't see it, you risk overdraft. This will help you gain better control and efficiency over your finances.

Microsoft Office Excel is the least expensive way to keep a balance on the computer. If you can't afford Microsoft Office on your computer do a Google search for "Open Office". Download that and use their "Calc" program, it is their version of Excel. It is a free open source program that does most of the basic things Microsoft Office does. They also have within their Office Suite a free version of PowerPoint, Word, and other programs. It's not pretty, it doesn't do everything, and you'll still wish you had Microsoft Office, but it gets the job done in this case if you don't have Microsoft Office or choose not to spend your money on it at this time.

~Excel~

Just start columns for each thing you need to track. Typically you only need: Date, Transaction, Amount,

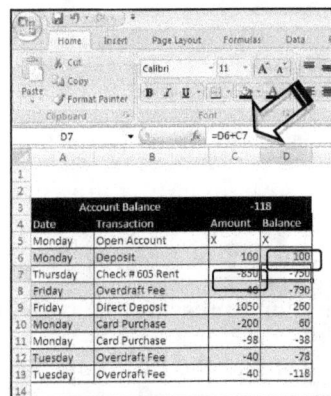

Balance, and Total. To add it all up at the top of the column over the dollar figure just use the sum formula[21]. The letter shows the vertical column and the number shows the horizontal row of the cell you are talking about. To see a running balance along the side after each transaction just add the cell above to the cell new cell. In this example cell "D6" is 100 plus cell "C7" which is -850. You must use the negative in front of all subtractions to make this method work. It is among the simpler ways to format your sheet.

---

[21] Example of sum formula "=SUM(C6:C13)" and "=D6+C7"

~Co Accounting~

If you are married, or otherwise responsible for the bills and income of more than one equally involved person, communication is key. You must find a way to keep the lines of communication open and this way all parties involved are aware of the state of the accounts. Almost without exception one person is a natural saver the other is a natural spender. If one person does all the banking there is bound to be tension. The banker of the family is likely to feel all the pressure of the bills and the rest of the family will go on oblivious to the situation and pressure the banker to lighten up because they want to spend the bill money on fun and food. If the banker of the family were to become in any way unable to participate, even if they are organized, the other person will be lost when bills are due.

Although we're still working on improving, my wife and I came up with a few ideas that have helped over the years. One of the best, since she is better organized and we are both busy, is that she gives the bills to me with instructions on who to pay and how much. Then I pay them with our online Bill Pay service. This way we both know what bills we're paying and the best part is that it opens the door of communication about finances.

$

13

DEBT

The "other side" of the bank is lending. This is actually the reason the bank exists. Without lending the bank would have virtually no income. The bank uses the savers money to lend it to the borrower. A case in point, Joe got his first credit card at 18 years old. He bought $1,500 in junk the first 6 months and only made the minimum $25 payments every month. 3 years later at 21 he was still using the card. He added more balance to it. As he kept up making the payment each month, the company added more available credit and he maxed that too. He was still making the minimum possible payment and most of his bill was from the original purchases he made back at 18 years old. The majority of his payments had gone to interest. Very little of it went to pay off the balance he used therefore he has a never ending balance.

So what is happening to Joe? Joe used his card for things he didn't need or should have saved for. He bought into a mindset that says: "You must borrow, you must have it NOW!"

Our 1st case study Robert lives in the same economy but doesn't have most of the concerns that Joe has. In fact, Robert is nearly completely free of any debt. He is also using the drop in the recent stock market to buy up good stocks from solid companies at low-low prices per share and knowing that they are likely to come back up eventually.

Banks and finance institutions use Roberts's cash to lend to Joe; the bank pays Robert for loaning them money to loan to Joe. AND Joe pays the whole bill.

~Debt: Good or Bad?~

Let's examine this as it has been a bone of contention in certain Christian circles. Borrowing can't be a sin. God told the Jews that He would make them lenders and not borrowers in Deuteronomy 28. God wouldn't make them lenders if borrowing was a sin. God won't be a part of helping someone sin. At the same time He said He would make them lenders not borrowers.

Evidentially God's ultimate plan for his people is to always be the ruling class. However, you borrow every time you turn your lights on. You use the electricity today but pay for it on your next months bill. So you must start where you are and take steps to move forward.

God has a billion ways to bring you a million dollars. Money is never an issue with God. But many of us have different levels of faith and understanding regarding money. You need to follow the Peace of God regarding your financial decisions, especially when it comes to debt. If you don't have peace on the inside, if you have a funny feeling in your gut that makes you uncomfortable regarding a decision you are about to make, you had better cancel it and take a step back. Used wisely any of the various tools offered by banks can be useful for you to leverage your time, money, and to improve your life quality. Used badly the loans will become a vice to crush you. Let's take a look at home buying for example.

~Rent VS Buy~

So should I rent or take out a mortgage loan and get a house? There are good calculators available online to help you determine your financial readiness for a home loan. What I want to examine here are the principles to consider when thinking about using credit.

When you rent, you are borrowing the apartment or house from the owner. Many times the owner has a mortgage so you are already paying a loan; it's just not your loan. The bible says that the borrower is servant to the lender[22] and anyone who has rented for any time knows that is true. By renting you borrow the house or apartment from the owner. The owners or managers come in often to update this, or inspect that. You are limited to what you can and cannot do to the property. Most won't even allow you to paint the walls yourself. They even call the owner a "land lord" The owner is the lord over your land.

On the other hand if you take out a mortgage you are now a borrower from the bank. You are servant to their terms and disclosures. The bank owns the house, but you are usually freer to do as you want than you would be in an apartment. The bank owns the house and has the right to foreclose on the house when you fail to pay. Of course so does the apartment.

Since the bible says to owe no man anything but to love him[23], you ought to believe God for a debt free house. As you are in the process of developing your faith for that you must decide which entity you are going to borrow from. The land lord or the bank? Both have merit.

If you are renting and God calls you to move to Africa you can pick up and go! If you "own" you must first sell your property or rent out the property to ensure

---

[22] Proverbs 22:7
[23] Romans 13:8

payments continue. Renting also gives you a lower commitment. Utilities are often included. Maintenance is usually preformed by the property owner. When something breaks you simply call them up and they fix it for you. Grass is mowed by the owners. You just pay your bill and go about your business. In some ways it's a care free life but a limited one.

If you know you are where you are supposed to be and God will not be moving you away any time soon, than the bank could give you a lower payment and a fixed payment which frees you up to serve in your local duties. This is because although rent may increase each year, typically your house payment is fixed and does not go up, however your property taxes could still increase your payment from time to time. You may also find that a house would give you more room for your growing family or ministry. Pray through the decision. God will help you determine which is best for you and which plan brings you into His perfect will for your life.

I like what one gentleman said: If you want to rent, fine, rent from the bank. We'll keep your rent payments fixed and in 30 years we'll give you the house for free! Of course you will want to be seeking God to get that house debt free faster, but it is a good point.

Follow these simple rules when considering taking a loan for a house (or any other need or project): Follow the Peace of God. Don't move if you have a sense of unease about it. Always seek a payment LOWER than you can afford. Houses have a way of taking on extra payments. Many apartments cover water, sewer, and trash, however as a home owner that is now your cost. Houses often have Home Owners Association Dues (HOA) which can be expensive. Pray until you have clear direction from God. Learn as much as you can about credit, credit scores, and the loan process before you jump in. Take courses for free online at various websites (see the resources at the back of this book). Get a firm grasp of the process you will go through if you "buy".

Romans 13:7-8 (NKJV) [7] *Render therefore to all their due: taxes to whom taxes are due, customs to whom customs, fear to whom fear, honor to whom honor.* [8] ***Owe no one anything except to love one another****, for he who loves another has fulfilled the law.*

The guiding principle found in Romans chapter 13 is not to owe anyone, or in other words do not allow yourself to get behind on your payments. If you have a tax bill due, pay it. If you have a light bill due, pay it. If you have an auto loan due, pay it. Don't get behind if it's in your power to do so.

Sometimes things happen, jobs are lost, or situations get beyond your immediate control. The grace of God will cover you and the Word of God will restore you. God's grace covers many things. It is for those very situations, in a fallen world system, He made provisions in both the old and new covenants to help people become debt free. The jubilee laws of Israel in the Mosaic Law were the very foundation of our bankruptcy laws in western societies. Lawyers studied the bible to help create these laws to remove debt from peoples' lives. If however it's in your ability to do so, make paying your bills a high priority. If you agree to something you had better make sure your word is your bond and you keep that promise. That's also known as integrity. If you expect God to honor His word to you, He expects to you to honor your word to Him and to others.

So you thought about it, researched it, and especially prayed about it and you've decided that God approves of you borrowing money for the specific task at hand. What products do the banks offer and which one is right for me?

~Secured VS Unsecured~

First of all, debt can be either secured or unsecured. This means that there may be something backing your debt or not. Secured means that something of value secures the loan. That something may be taken by the bank in repayment if you default (don't pay). Unsecured means that nothing secures the loan other than your word and credit history. Therefore nothing can be directly taken in repayment, but could still be taken through levies and court actions in collections should you not repay.

~Open VS Closed~

Really there are two basic categories of lending; all of which can be either secured or unsecured. Open ended credit (also called revolving credit) and close ended credit (also called non-revolving credit). With revolving credit you use it and pay it back then use it and pay it back over and over as long as the account is open. With non-revolving credit you borrow a specific amount for a specific purpose and make specific payments back overtime. Once paid off the loan closes and you have to apply all over again if you want more money. These loans have a fixed payment, usually fixed interest, and scheduled payoff date. As long as you make all payments on time, you could know 5 years from now what you will be paying and when it will be paid off entirely.

~Credit Cards~

Two examples of open credit are credit cards and lines of credit. You use your credit cards and then get a bill. Typically if you pay your entire bill before the due date then you pay no interest. If you do not pay the entire bill, you pay interest on all or part of this statement's balance if you don't pay off the entire balance. Check with your bank. Interest rates on credit cards are variable and usually high. They are often negotiable as long as you make all payments on time and never use more than your credit limit at any one time. But this is getting harder in recent years. The best for your standing with the bank is to pay off your entire balance every month. This gives you more favor then leaving small balances and not paying in full.

~Lines of Credit~

A line of credit is similar to a loan. A credit limit is set from which you can borrow and pay back over and over again similar to a credit card. You can write checks from a line of credit or have portions of your available credit transferred to your checking account. Typically you pay interest on any balance owed for as long as you use it, like a loan. If you use it for 3 days and pay it back you pay 3 days of interest. The interest rates tend to be more stable than a credit card and you will generally find these to be a better option for actually borrowing money. The rates are still variable and could go up or down over time.

~Using Open Credit~

Use Credit Cards for daily spending and take advantage of the rewards programs. Never carry a balance as interest rates on these can skyrocket overnight with little to no warning. Always pay the balance in full each month or cut it up. If you purchase everything through your credit card and make one payment each month to pay it off, this could maximize your rewards while decreasing the amount of debit card transactions. This makes checking balances easier to keep up with.

A note to be made on this, your limit is generally your limit per statement cycle. If you have a $3,000 credit limit, you use it and pay it off twice in the month of March, the credit card company says that you have used $6,000 which is twice your limit. It doesn't matter that you paid it off so that you never had a balance over your limit. This can be considered a red flag for potential money laundering and is taken seriously by the banks. They may even block or close your card over it. Pay your bill off after you get it, and use no more than your limit within that month and you should avoid this troublesome phone call.

A Line of credit makes sense for someone who will need to borrow money from time to time, more than once without knowing how much or for how long. The interest rates will be variable but usually tied to something like the Prime Rate. Therefore they are more stable and usually only raise when the Prime Rate[24] changes. One use for a line of credit may be to have a reserve of emergency funds in case you need to make repairs to a car or home. Some have used these funds to carry themselves through tough times after injury or losing a job. Some use the money to invest in a project or business. Some people use $20,000 for two months and pay it off, and then borrow it again latter for another short term business opportunity. The best time to apply for a line of credit is when you don't need one. Usually the circumstances that cause you to want a line of credit prevent you from qualifying for one.

~Loans~

Closed ended credit is most often just called a loan. In taking a loan you borrow a specified amount for a

---

[24] http://www.bankrate.com/rates/interest-rates/prime-rate.aspx

specified time, usually at a fixed rate. 4 popular loans of this type are:

1. Home Mortgage
2. Home Equity Loan
3. Personal Loan
4. Auto Loan

Home equity and auto loans represent secured loans. The home or auto secures the loan and if you fail to make payments the bank can take it back. Personal loans are unsecured which means they are based only on your word and credit history. Unsecured loans can have higher interest, however they may be better because if life turns on you the home, auto and property you have is safer from creditors. Secured loans could be a financially wiser move given that the interest rates are so much lower, which is less money out of your pocket long term.

~Using Open Ended Credit~

The bottom line with credit is this: Proceed with Caution. A credit card can be convenient, it can even leverage your purchasing power through rewards points programs. However never ever carry a balance always pay them off in full every month. If you have not developed the discipline to do so, call the card company close it and cut it up.

Loans and lines can be useful. If you have a sizable down payment for a big purchase like home/auto/business but need that extra to put you over. However, buyer beware, the loan should be well thought through.

I once bought a minivan. I needed a new larger vehicle because I was transporting to full sized adults and a car seat in a small pickup truck with a single cab and a bench seat. I bought late at night, with no real plan or research. I bought feeling pressured and ended up buying a car way out of my price range. Emotion is a bad reason to enter any contract. Emotion can never be allowed to interfere with a financial purchase. Have emotions but never let emotions have you. A loan is a contract with another party. You will be bound to them until it is repaid or forgiven. Make sure you really want to be bound with that party, that institution, that payment, that rate, and that amount. Take your time, pray, research, gather facts. Make sure you understand exactly what you are buying and why. Do not sign until you are at total peace with the deal. Even right to the last minute you are better off running away from the situation, praying overnight, and coming back than you are signing it without total peace. A great rule of thumb here: "Any big decision should be able to wait 48 hours."

$

14

FICO

W hat is a FICO score? Many people want to know what a FICO score is. FICO stands for the Fair Isaac Corporation, founded in 1956 and in 2009 renamed: FICO. This is the one company that has more control over your interest rates and loan approvals than any other. They review your credit reports and create a score based on the information found there.

The formula that determines that score is TOP SECRET. The banks don't even know it. We do know a few things about the score though. The Credit Scores can vary from 300 to 850, recently information has come out that it may go into the 900's now. A "Good Score" is hard to determine because different lenders have different cut off marks. According to Wikipedia the average marker in the USA is about 640.[25] This score is about the breaking point between bad and good. Typically, though, banks are looking for scores in the 700's

---

[25] http://en.wikipedia.org/wiki/Subprime_lending

~DSR or DTI~

The better your score the better the interest rate and the higher the chance your loan is approved. The score isn't the only factor in approving loans. Many people with HIGH credit scores are turned down due to a high debt to income ration, known as DTI. This is also known as Debt Service Ration or DSR. The following are the categories that FICO uses and the percentages showing the importance of each category. This information was taken directly from www.myfico.com[26]; payment history 35% (Were you late or on time?), amounts Owed 30%, length of credit history 15%, new credit 10%, and types of credit used 10%.

If you pay all of your bills on time and you are never late you have overcome half of the battle with FICO. Another thing to keep in mind is history. It is recommended that you keep between one to three credit cards and no more. Keep one for as long as possible. This history factor doesn't so much take into account the old closed accounts you have in your history as much as it wants to see the oldest account you have that is still currently open. If you

---

[26] http://www.myfico.com/CreditEducation/

are closing out credit card accounts keep the one that has been open the longest.

~Pay On Time~

Pay your bills on time. If it has already been charged off to collections realize that paying off collections will not remove it from your credit report, it will stay there for seven years. The seven year period starts at the last date of contact or payment[27]. If it has been 6 years and you call them about anything your seven years could start over. Additionally the creditor could sell your debt to another collector and that could restart their clock too. There is much more too it than this so seek a reputable credit counselor if you have trouble making payments. If you believe it has been more than 7 years since the you last dealt with the debt you should dispute it with the credit reporting agency under the Fair Credit Reporting Act (FCRA) and a clause known as Date of Last Contact/Activity (DOLA). Of course you should pay if you are able.

~Low Balances~

Keep balances low on credit cards and all open revolving credit. Never use more than 45% of the available

---

[27] http://consumerist.com/2007/04/negative-items-fall-off-credit-report-after-seven-year-itch-as-long-as-you-dont-scratch-em-creditors.html

credit. This means that if you have a credit card that has a spending limit of $5,000 you never want to use more than $2,250 of that limit. Simply take your limit and multiply that by 0.45 to find out how much you can actually use. If you go over from time to time it's OK, but not if you are trying to take out a large loan soon and not on a regular basis. You should be paying it off in full every month anyway, even if you are using no more than 45% of your limit. Do not close cards just to raise your credit score and do not move money around from card to card. Just pay it off. Closing cards because you have too many, however, can be a good thing long term. Again seek an experienced reputable credit counselor on this.

The only time moving money around in balance transfers is good is if that helps you consolidate your bills into one place with a lower interest. This may not help your score short term; but it will help you pay it all off faster which affects your score long term. Keep no more than 3 credit cards at any given time open. If you want to close your card once it has been paid off make sure to call and close the card. Don't assume that it will close just because you paid it to a zero balance. It looks better if you close the card than if the credit card company closes it due to inactivity.

~New Credit~

New accounts can lower your credit score and a rapid build up of credit accounts is a big red flag! Open one to two credit cards over time and no more, keep them and use them wisely as stated above.

Research, Research, Research. Make sure you are in the right loan or card for you. Pull your own credit first before looking, this doesn't count against your score. Use credit responsibly, here are a few tips. Apply for new credit accounts only as needed. Use it correctly. Closing an account does not make it go away. It stays on the report 7 years. Paying off collections doesn't make the account fall off of your credit report or improve your score all that much if any; but may have legal and or long term benefits. The Word of God says to owe no man anything but love. Therefore you should always seek to pay your' debts. It also laid the foundation of our bankrucpty laws clearing debts and offering a start over. Allow the Spirit to lead you in your decisions regarding past debt.

Fixed payment and fixed term loans are often better than open revolving credit. Have five or less open credit accounts on your file and make sure that only two of them are revolving accounts like credit cards or lines of credit. Pay loans on time and pay credit cards off in full each month. Use no more than 45% of your credit cards/LOC available limits.

~Deeper Look at DSR or DTI~

Here is a quick look at DTI/DSR and the loan approval systems that are out there. The concept of DTI (Debt To Income), also known as DSR (Debt Service Ratio), is summarized as the amount of debt the person has compared to the amount of income they bring in and how they use it all. A person has a better chance of getting approved for credit products when they don't need them because they have the income to support the debt.

If the person looses their job they often want to apply for credit to help out during the time it takes to find a new job. By that time it's too late because their DTI is higher without income or on unemployment income. If you feel that you would in the future desire to have a line of credit for emergencies, apply ahead of time before you would actually need it. Its irony, those who don't need it usually qualify over those who do.

Debt to income is a formula. Debt divided by income. An Example helps here.

~Example of DSR or DTI~

Company	Starting Limit	Balance	Payment
ABC Mortgage	$225,000.00	$200,000.00	$1,200.00
Auto Loan	$25,000.00	$19,000.00	$600.00
Credit Card	$7,000.00	$6,000.00	$200.00
Credit Card	$5,000.00	$3,500.00	$150.00
TOTAL	**$262,000.00**	**$228,500.00**	**$2,150.00**

The first section for open credit reflects available limits and for closed credit reflects the original loan amount. The balance is the current balance on the account. This will be the balance at the time the credit was last reported. It doesn't matter if you pay your balance in full every month, this will be used to calculate your DTI this is one of the reasons you want to keep your card balances under 45% of the limit.

The payment section will show the payments you've been making. If there is no payment: such as a credit card you haven't used or a student loan that's being differed the creditor may calculate a payment that could be due. This is in order to figure out if you could afford the new credit AND the existing credit.

TOTAL	**$262,000.00**	**$228,500.00**	**$2,150.00**

Let's say that the person in the example above makes $45,000 a year. The lender will take that and divide it by 12. This gives the borrower $3,750 per month. Lender usually uses GROSS income, before taxes, because it's really not their business what two people making the same amount choose to deduct for health insurance or other deductions. This person has a debt payment of $2150. So $2150/$3750 = 57.3% This person has a **Debt To Income (DTI/DSR) of 57.3%**. Most lenders require less than 45-50%. Markets change and lenders vary on this, but this is the concept they are addressing.

~Usage~

They may also take a look at your usage. This comes from taking your available credit on open lines and figuring out how much you use. This is where keeping your credit card balances low even if you pay them in full every month comes into play. Line usage refers to the amount of your open line limits that you use. In this persons case they have $9,500 in credit card balances and $12,000 total available limits. $9,500/$12,000=79.2%

That is 79.2% line usage. Lenders usually like to see less than 45% Line usage.

Credit Card	$7,000.00	$6,000.00	$200.00
Credit Card	$5,000.00	$3,500.00	$150.00
Total Line	**$12,000.00**	**$9,500.00**	**$350.00**

~Balances~

Another factor that they look at when lending is balance in use. Lenders like to see that only a certain percentage of a person's annual salary is tied up in open line balances. The general rule is less than 25-30% of the annual salary should be tied up in line balances. If the person above makes $45,000 per year that means 25% of their income is $11,250. They are using $9,500 of their open credit. Therefore this person is using 21% of their income on line balances, ($9,500/$45,000=0.211) which is less than 25% of their income on open revolving lines.

~Example Person's Results~

To review, this person has: DTI/DSR: 57.3%, usage of: 79.2%, total balance in use of 21% of annual salary.

Even if the persons FICO is good and they have been with their employer longer than 2 years, the lender may still see the DTI/DSR and usage as too high of a risk and may decline the loan.

This is how a person with a good FICO score and great income can still be declined on a loan/line request. I hope this helps you to understand the approval process better and begin to plan your finances to match up to this type of scrutiny. The lender is essentially asking one question: "Is this person a risk?"

If you aren't sure what your credit score or credit report looks like, you can always get them through the following resources and many other places:

- www.MyFico.com
- www.annualcreditreport.com
- Identity Theft Protection Services
  - Usually offer credit score tracking
- The "Big Three" credit bureaus.
  - Experian
  - Equifax
  - TransUnion

$

14

Conclusion

So now that you have all that information on banking and finances, what's next? What are you going to do different? You know what a checking is, how items post, and how to keep a record. You know a little more about credit and debt. You know a little more about planning for retirement and investing. What's next?

If you aren't a tither, that would be the first place to start. Malachi chapter 3 points out that the devourer comes to kill our financial crops. By tithing you stop that devourer. Non tithers often say things like: "It seems like I put my money into pockets with holes in them." Start by putting aside the money and paying your tithe. Open a separate account and have your paycheck auto deducted for the amount needed. That is the first step toward financial freedom.

~Goals~

You need to set goals. What do you want to accomplish in the next 6 months, 1 year, and 5 years. You really don't need to be that specific at first. Just make a list of everything you want to accomplish in life. Put a time frame next to it if you have one. Feel free to have an unknown amount of time on large dreams. Also, don't be discouraged if it takes longer than you planned, just keep going forward. Maybe you are dreaming of something but have no idea how long it will take, that is fine. Just set goals. I have a friend who once made a simple list of everything he currently wanted to see happen in his life. There were goals about marriage, jobs, places he wanted to see, etc. Within 2 years he pulled that out one day and realized all the items had been accomplished. It's not so much about setting out a plan to make it happen; just the act of making goals will set your mind and spirit to working them out. You could even post the goals on the wall by your door, then everyday read them to yourself and say: "I receive that!"

~Taken Action~

Take action. That is the most important part of making changes. If you have been overdrawn a lot in the past, or maybe you are right now, take the examples given earlier. Close out the account and deal with cash, or put away the card and checks, and deal with money orders. If you are not keeping a detailed record start one. If you want to know more about investing, get a book, do some Google searches and learn more. If you need to start saving; start by putting aside as little as $1 or $5 a paycheck. Use a jar at home if you can't find a free savings account. Once you have saved the amount needed to keep the minimum balance, usually $300, open the savings with it. Some banks now offer plans that transfer money to your savings every time you use your card. Be creative.

You should have giving goals. I want to give this item, or that amount, by the end of the year. I've set a goal of giving away a debt free car. I did it once. I now have a goal of taking someone to a car lot and letting them pick the one they want. I'm not there yet, but I'm working toward that.

Have goals regarding your lively hood or calling. What has God called you to do? If you don't know what your calling is yet, just consider what you are good at. It probably has something to do with it. Work toward your talents and passions. Make small attainable goals. If you play guitar, learn a new song, work through a book that teaches you a new skill set or style. If you are a computer person, buy a new program, or learn a new set of codes. Attend a seminar or class that touches on your passion.

Whatever your station in life, take an hour, or even a day, to pray and ponder, what your goals ought to be. Make simple, attainable goals. If you have a large dream, break it up into smaller pieces. You want to own a multimillion dollar restaurant? Great! Go get your business license, research what you need. What is the cost of the building, the equipment the upkeep? Take steps, don't worry about the money to start it, at first. If you start taking steps and working toward it, God will bring the increase if it's His passion that has been birthed inside of you. The journey of a thousand miles begins with a single step. Go stepping.

Section IV

Supplements

$

16

CALCULATIONS

~Exercise: Math Time~

The money earned in a Savings/CD or for that matter the interest you pay on a loan is calculated by most banks using a formula called daily compounding. This is the formula to compute compounded interest for one month:

(BALANCE) X (RATE) X (DAYS IN STATEMENT CYCLE)

---

(365)

Robert put in $2,000 of his own money. In order to calculate this we must know how to turn a percentage into a decimal figure. To do this simply take the decimal point and move it two spaces to the left. For example 10 % is the number 10.00. Then move the point to the left two spaces which is now 0.10.

As for statement cycles, most statement cycles will vary between 28-36 days. Short months, such as February will be less, and long months that include more weekends and holidays may be longer. However for our purposes we will use an average. The average month is 30 days. There are 365 days in a year.

~Example of Roberts IRA~

($2,000 X 0.10 X 30)÷365 = $16.44 Per Month

Robert only earned $16.44 the first month. If you took this amount times 12 months you get $197.28 for the first Year. If you then take that and multiply it by 18 years you only get $3,551.04. At a linear rate of growth he would have only earned $3,551.04 for 18 years worth of investment. So where did the growth come from? How did Robert gain over $48,000? That is where compounding comes in to play. The first month he earned $16.44. The next month his balance was $2016.44. So now you plug the new balance into the same equation and you get $16.57. ($2016.44 X 0.10 X 30)÷365 = $16.57

So the second month he's already earning more than the first month. As this process rolls on and on over the months and years the amounts will eventually get exponentially larger. The bottom line of compounding is: Your interest earns interest. This is one way to make your money work for you.

$

17

FDIC

W hat is the FDIC and what does it mean for a
bank to be FDIC insured? This has been a
major topic of discussion in the last few
years. With the market crashes and banking fiascoes of
2008 and beyond people are asking more questions about
FDIC.

The following is directly from their site:[28]

*"What does the FDIC do? The Federal Deposit
Insurance Corporation (FDIC) preserves and promotes
public confidence in the U.S. financial system by insuring
deposits in banks and thrift institutions for up to $250,000;
by identifying, monitoring and addressing risks to the
deposit insurance funds; and by limiting the effect on the
economy and the financial system when a bank or thrift
institution fails."*

FDIC stands for Federal Deposit Insurance
Corporation. They provide deposit insurance for customers
of failed banks. If a bank fails and closes, or if the Federal

---

[28] http://www.fdic.gov/help/faq.html

Reserve closes them for compliance failures the FDIC covers $250,000 per person per institution and separately $250,000 per IRA customer per institution.

~FDIC VS Fraud~

FDIC does not cover fraud. If fraud occurs on your bank accounts it is up to each individual bank to provide their own policy about it. Some banks will give you credit for anything fraudulent that clears your account. Other banks actually may hold you responsible for the first $100 or $500 of fraud on your accounts. You want to know which is true for your bank. If you are not sure ask your bank for literature on their fraud policy, this can usually be found in your disclosures.

~Who is covered?~

The FDIC covers an individual not an account. It doesn't matter if you have 1 account with a bank or 50 accounts with a bank. The total of all your accounts with each bank are covered up to the current FDIC limit "Per Person - Per Entity". The only way to get more than the FDIC limit by yourself is to open accounts at multiple banks. Another way is for an investment advisor through your brokerage firm who can open CD's through other banks for you. These are often called brokered CD's and usually have FDIC coverage. The benefit of doing it this way is that you know someone has done all the shopping for you to get the highest rates available and that the one person can service all the accounts yet each banks FDIC limits can cover you individually. Therefore you can get ALL or MOST of your money covered by one investment advisor by that advisor spreading the money across multiple banks.

A married person should want to hold all their accounts in joint ownership, unless you have extenuating circumstances. If all accounts are held jointly the FDIC coverage is twice what it would be alone. Remember the coverage is per person per bank. So make sure that all accounts are titled as joint accounts to make sure all are covered. That way together you have twice the coverage. If the limit per person per bank is $250,000, than with two people you have $500,000.

Another way to add coverage is by adding beneficiaries to your account. You can add another $250,000 in coverage per beneficiary. A beneficiary is someone who will inherent your money if you die. However the titling on this has to be exactly as the FDIC wants it to appear. You will want to check with the FDIC directly on this. Call 411 for their number or check their website at www.fdic.gov. In addition to the beneficiary information you can also find on their website an "Electronic Deposit Insurance Estimator". This tool helps you determine if all your funds are insured. There are also two guides that can be found that will help you understand more about the FDIC as it relates to your deposits. The two guides are: "Insuring your deposits" and "Your insured deposits". Check these as well as the rest of their website for more information.

Retirement accounts, such as IRA's are separately insured. This means that in addition to your normal money you can have an additional $250,000 in coverage through your IRA. For example you could have a total of $250,000 in your checking and savings, and another $250,000 in your IRA all covered. This applies to money you contribute to your IRA each year, but it's also a good way of insuring your other retirement money. If you are reaching or have reached the age of retirement and the market looks bad or you have left your job, you can roll all or part of your 401K (which is typically invested in the market in Non-FDIC products) into your FDIC insured IRA at the bank. This way you can guarantee your money is safer. There is no need to keep the funds separate from the IRA you already have in most cases, consult your tax advisor to be sure.

You can use the FDIC online calculator to determine your current coverage. Be prepared to put in a lot of personal information like accounts numbers and amounts. If you don't feel confident in doing this you can read all their terms and use a paper and pencil to calculate it yourself. FDIC: Electronic Deposit Insurance Calculator[29]

---

[29] https://www.fdic.gov/edie/index.html

$

18

PRIVACY

While we are talking about the government and their regulations let's also talk quickly about Privacy. The government, Federal and State, has passed many laws on privacy. You have the right not to be called, mailed, emailed or otherwise contacted for sales reasons if you choose. There is even a "Do not call" registry[30] you can add yourself to. The registry is a national list of people who have "opted out" of getting sales calls. Companies must legally "scrub" their phone lists every so often to account for new numbers that have been added to the list. Adding your name to the registry does not stop ALL sales calls, and does not stop them from calling right away. As time goes on businesses will add your name to their do not call list and stop calling. Also, if a bank or company already has you as a customer then they can ignore this list for you and contact you anyway unless you call or notify that institution not to. They can ignore the list

---

[30] https://www.donotcall.gov/

because you have chosen to establish a relationship with that institution and therefore calling you is a way to service you as a customer. Anyone you have or had service with may call you for service reasons. If these service calls turn into sales calls its ok. They may not call you strictly for sales if you said not to.

~Do Not Call List~

The upside to adding your name to this list is that you will get less and less of the sales calls offering you silly things. The downside is that the bank may not be able to call you any more when new products or services come out. You will then need to take even more responsibility to keep up to date with your accounts. Your bank can and is required to provide you with information about their privacy policies and what they do to keep your information from getting into the wrong hands. Read these disclosures to understand what your company is doing.

Many companies have done away with sharing your information with other companies. There used to be a day before the advent of "identity theft" that companies actually sold each other the names and contact info of each others customers to broaden their search for new customers. Too many factors have made this a rare practice these days. But just in case you want to be sure that your bank isn't doing this you can read their privacy disclosures and notify them of your preferences.

~Partners~

Selling to third parties and sharing with partners are NOT the same thing. Just because a company doesn't "sell" information to third parties looking for leads, doesn't mean it doesn't "work with" other companies to provide you options and therefore has them offer you things on their behalf. For Example: Debit Card Programs, such as travel rewards are rarely offered by the bank directly. Some company that specializes in those services offers them to the banks customers for them. You may be contacted by a company offering you a service attached to your debit card, offering you a free trial. These companies weren't SOLD your information, they were given your information so that they could offer you a service on the banks behalf.

~What to consider~

If you opt out, and decide to ask you're bank not to call for any solicitation (fancy word for sales) that is fine. However banks frequently change their products and services and you are required to keep up to date with what the bank offers so that you know you are not paying too much for one product or missing out on a free service from another. Interest rates decline on outdated products too, so you should call your bank once a year to find out what products are being offered and if yours are out of date. You could even say: "My account has a solicitation preference, however I want you this once to tell me what products and services you offer that I am not taking advantage of." Maybe nothing will come of it. You never know, maybe there is some new amazing thing you've been missing out on. I've had a few people tell me they wished someone told them sooner. You could also research it all online if you desire on their website.

Resources

Financial Vision

Many times having a clear vision of your goals is a good place to start. Use the following to make your own financial Vision and Mission Statements!

VISION: *I see myself fully supplied in every area of my life so that I can give to every good work. I see myself debt free. I see myself taking new ground every day.*

MISSION: *I will help my Vision come to pass by taking control over my spending, and utilizing the financial tools given to me. I will take action to prevent myself from paying unnecessary fees. I will put money aside for Tithe AND Offering. I will put money into my Savings Account. I will be a good steward over my money and make wise purchases. I will make sure my savings money is getting the best possible rate of return. I will pay down and pay off debt, aggressively! I will make wise decisions in borrowing and credit, by planning ahead, researching, and taking my time before making a decision.*

CONFESSION: *I call myself supplied, to the full, until it overflows onto others around me! I call myself debt free! I call myself a supplier of others needs, wants, and desires! I am God's distribution center to meet the needs of others!*

Vision Scriptures

2 Corinthians 9

[8] And God is able to make all grace abound toward you, that you, always having all sufficiency in all things, may have an abundance for every good work.

Matthew 25

[23] His lord said to him, 'Well done, good and faithful servant; you have been faithful over a few things, I will make you ruler over many things. Enter into the joy of your lord.'

Genesis 1

[28] Then God blessed them, and God said to them, "Be fruitful and multiply; fill the earth and subdue it; have dominion over the fish of the sea, over the birds of the air, and over every living thing that moves on the earth."

Deuteronomy 28

[12] The LORD will open to you His good treasure, the heavens, to give the rain to your land in its season, and to bless all the work of your hand. You shall lend to many nations, but you shall not borrow.

Romans 13

[8] Owe no one anything except to love one another, for he who loves another has fulfilled the law.

Genesis 18

[18] Abraham will surely become a great and powerful nation, and all nations on earth will be blessed through him.

Galations 3

9 So then those who are of faith are blessed with believing Abraham.

Offering Confession

Used by EMIC 2010:

As we give today's tithe and offerings we believe we receive:

- Jobs or Better Jobs
- Raises and Bonuses
- Benefits
- Sales and Commissions
- Estates and Inheritances
- Interest and Income
- Rebates and Returns
- Checks in the mail
- Gifts and Suprises
- Lost money found
- Bills Paid Off
- Debts Demolished
- And Royalties Received.

This is my year of overflow! I expect more out of heaven than ever before. I receive my harvest by faith in Jesus Name!

Websites

The Following are Helpful Resources:

Banking:

- www.crown.org
- www.daveramsey.com
- www.handsonbanking.org
- www.irs.gov
- www.federalreserve.gov
    - Helpful free E-book of a similar nature by the Federal Reserve

        http://www.bos.frb.org/education/pubs/banking2.pdf
- www.myfico.com
    - http://www.myfico.com/crediteducation/
- www.annualcreditreport.com

Ministry and Bible Principles:

- www.KCM.org
- www.JDM.org
- www.JerrySavelle.org
- www.EMIC.org
- www.crown.org

About the Author

 I was introduced to Kenneth Copeland Ministries in 2003 through the West Coast Believer's Conventions and a book called "The Laws of Prosperity" by KCM. After learning that finances were important to God and a definite part of God's plan for all His children, I made it a point to learn more about it and take that knowledge to others. I am married to a wonderful and supportive wife with two amazing and talented children. For more than 5 years I've researched and studied wealth and how to handle it. With on the job experience in the financial industry I have helped many people who were interested in learning more about money and banking. Many times I was asked if I would write a book, so I did! Through this book I am fulfilling my mission and calling which is to help people succeed; spiritually, physically, financially, and in all areas of life.

Bulldog Publications
Darrell Glen Wolfe, Author